D1191687

AMERICA'S WARS THROUGH PRIMARY SOURCES

Primary Source Accounts of the

Civil War

Manville Public Library
Manville, New Jersey

ARCHIE P. McDONALD

MyReportLinks.com Books

an imprint of

 Enslow Publishers, Inc.

Box 398, 40 Industrial Road
Berkeley Heights, NJ 07922
USA

MyReportLinks.com Books, an imprint of Enslow Publishers, Inc. MyReportLinks® is a registered trademark of Enslow Publishers, Inc.

Library of Congress Cataloging-in-Publication Data

McDonald, Archie P.
  Primary source accounts of the Civil War / Archie P. McDonald.
      p. cm. — (America's wars through primary sources)
  Includes bibliographical references and index.
  ISBN 1-59845-000-X
  1. United States—History—Civil War, 1861–1865—Sources—Juvenile literature. I. Title. II. Series.
  E464.M38 2006
  973.7—dc22
                                    2005014052

Printed in the United States of America

10 9 8 7 6 5 4 3 2 1

To Our Readers:
Through the purchase of this book, you and your library gain access to the Report Links that specifically back up this book.
The Publisher will provide access to the Report Links that back up this book and will keep these Report Links up to date on **www.myreportlinks.com** for five years from the book's first publication date.
We have done our best to make sure all Internet addresses in this book were active and appropriate when we went to press. However, the author and the Publisher have no control over, and assume no liability for, the material available on those Internet sites or on other Web sites they may link to.
The usage of the MyReportLinks.com Books Web site is subject to the terms and conditions stated on the Usage Policy Statement on **www.myreportlinks.com.**
A password may be required to access the Report Links that back up this book. The password is found on the bottom of page 4 of this book.
Any comments or suggestions can be sent by e-mail to comments@myreportlinks.com or to the address on the back cover.

Photo Credits: Bartleby.com, p. 112; Civil War Net, p. 97; Documenting the American South, the University of North Carolina, p. 70; Enslow Publishers, Inc., pp. 8, 19, 28; 25; Kentucky Education Television, p. 36; Library of Congress, pp. 1, 3, 7, 9, 11, 13, 15, 21, 23, 25, 26, 30, 35, 56, 61, 64, 66, 68, 73, 76, 79, 80, 94, 101, 104, 107, 110, 111; MyReportLinks.com Books, p. 4; National Archives and Records Administration, pp. 45, 50, 57, 99; National Park Service, pp. 16, 41, 48, 54, 85, 96; PBS, p. 38; Photos.com (flag background), p. 1, 3, 5-7; Poetry and Music of the War Between the States, p. 82; Rice University, p. 75; Robert E. Lee Papers, Special Collections, Leyburn Library, Washington and Lee University, Lexington, Virginia, pp. 42, 43; Smithsonian Institution, pp. 53, 91, 105; The Avalon Project at Yale Law School, p. 33; The Gilder Lehrman Institute of American History/The Chicago Historical Society, p. 89; The Historical *New York Times* Project, p. 103; The University of Virginia, pp. 62, 93; Tulane University, p. 31; Virginia Military Institute, p. 59.

Cover Photo: Library of Congress.

Every effort has been made to locate all copyright holders of material used in this book. If any errors or omissions have occurred, please contact us at www.myreportlinks.com. We will try to make corrections in future editions.

CONTENTS

MyReportLinks.com Books
Great Books, Great Links, Great for Research!

The Internet sites featured in this book can save you hours of research time. These Internet sites—we call them **"Report Links"**—are constantly changing, but we keep them up to date on our Web site.

When you see this "Approved Web Site" logo, you will know that we are directing you to a great Internet site that will help you with your research.

Give it a try! Type http://www.myreportlinks.com into your browser, click on the series title and enter the password, then click on the book title, and scroll down to the Report Links listed for this book.

The Report Links will bring you to great source documents, photographs, and illustrations. MyReportLinks.com Books save you time, feature Report Links that are kept up to date, and make report writing easier than ever! A complete listing of the Report Links can be found on pages 114–115 at the back of the book.

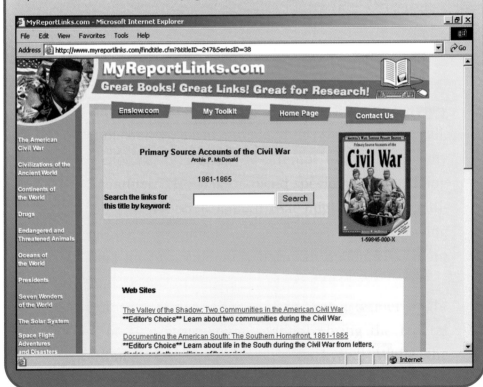

Please see "To Our Readers" on the copyright page for important information about this book, the MyReportLinks.com Web site, and the Report Links that back up this book.

Please enter **PCW1618** if asked for a password.

WHAT ARE PRIMARY SOURCES?

September 2, 1862

Dear Wife,
Kiss the Baby for me and Write as soon as you get this. . . . when I write again
I suppose I shall tell you if I am spared how being on a battle feels.

— Private John Pardington, 24th Michigan Volunteers,
in a letter to his wife, Sarah.

The young Union soldier who wrote these words never dreamed that they would be read by anyone but his wife. They were not intended to be read as a history of the Civil War. But his words—and the words of others that have come down to us through scholars or were saved over generations by family members—are unique resources. Historians call such writings primary source documents. As you read this book, you will find other primary source accounts of the war written by the men and women who fought it. Their letters home reflect their thoughts, their dreams, their fears, and their longing for loved ones. Some of them speak of the excitement of battle, while others mention the everyday boredom of day-to-day life in camp.

But the story of a war is not only the story of the men and women in service. This book also contains diary entries, newspaper accounts, official documents, speeches, and songs of the war years. They reflect the opinions of those who were not in battle but who were still affected by the war. All of these things as well as photographs and art can be considered primary sources—they were created by people who participated in, witnessed, or were affected by the events of the time.

Many of these sources, such as letters and diaries, are a reflection of personal experience. Others, such as newspaper accounts, reflect the mood of the time as well as the opinions of the papers' editors. All of them give us a unique insight into history as it happened. But it is also important to keep in mind that each source reflects its author's biases, beliefs, and background. Each is still someone's interpretation of an event.

Some of the primary sources in this book will be easy to understand; others may not. Their authors came from a different time and were products of different backgrounds and levels of education. So as you read their words, you will see that some of those words may be spelled differently than we would spell them. And some of their stories may be written without the kinds of punctuation you are used to seeing. Each source has been presented as it was originally written, but wherever a word or phrase is unclear or might be misunderstood, an explanation has been added.

TIME LINE OF THE CIVIL WAR

1860—NOVEMBER 6: Republican Abraham Lincoln is elected president of the United States.

—DECEMBER 20: South Carolina enacts ordinance of secession. Within about six weeks, Florida, Georgia, Alabama, Louisiana, Mississippi, and Texas also secede.

1861—FEBRUARY 9: Delegates from the seven seceded states meet in Montgomery, Alabama, to write a constitution for the Confederate States of America.

—FEBRUARY 18: Jefferson Davis is inaugurated provisional president of the Confederate States of America and is later confirmed by election as president.

—MARCH 4: Abraham Lincoln is inaugurated president of the United States.

—APRIL 12: Confederates commanded by General P.G.T. Beauregard fire on Fort Sumter, located in Charleston Harbor, commanded by Major Robert Anderson.

—APRIL 15: Lincoln calls for seventy-five thousand volunteers to put down the rebellion in South Carolina. Two days later, four more states secede—Arkansas, North Carolina, Tennessee, and Virginia—and subsequently become part of the Confederacy.

—JULY 21: The Confederate command of General P.G.T. Beauregard defeats Union general Irwin McDowell's army at Bull Run, or Manassas, in Virginia, in the first major battle of the war. First notice of General T. J. Jackson, who "stood like a stonewall" and stopped the Union offensive.

1862—JUNE 1: Robert E. Lee is given command of the Army of Northern Virginia.

—SEPTEMBER 17: General Lee's army fights the Battle of Antietam, or Sharpsburg, in Maryland, against the army commanded by General George Brinton McClellan, and then returns to Virginia, ending Lee's first attempt to invade the Union. This battle is the bloodiest single day of fighting in the Civil War. Soon afterward, President Abraham Lincoln issues the preliminary Emancipation Proclamation.

1863—JANUARY 1: The Emancipation Proclamation, which promises freedom to slaves in those states still in rebellion, goes into effect.

—MAY 1–4: Lee achieves his greatest tactical victory of the war against General Joseph Hooker at the Battle of Chancellorsville, but at great loss: the wounding on May 2 and death eight days later of General T. J. "Stonewall" Jackson.

—JULY 1–3: The Battle of Gettysburg is fought, marking a turning point in the war as the Union army stops Lee's second invasion of the North.

—JULY 4: General Ulysses S. Grant captures Vicksburg, Mississippi, which allows the Union to control the Mississippi River for the remainder of the war.

1864—SEPTEMBER 2: General William T. Sherman takes possession of Atlanta, Georgia.

—NOVEMBER 8: President Lincoln is reelected.

—NOVEMBER 15: General William T. Sherman begins his "March to the Sea," from Atlanta to Savannah, Georgia.

1865—APRIL 9: General Lee surrenders what is left of the Army of Northern Virginia to General Ulysses S. Grant at Appomattox Courthouse, Virginia. Other Confederate units surrender soon afterward.

—APRIL 14: President Lincoln is assassinated by John Wilkes Booth at Ford's Theatre in Washington, D.C.

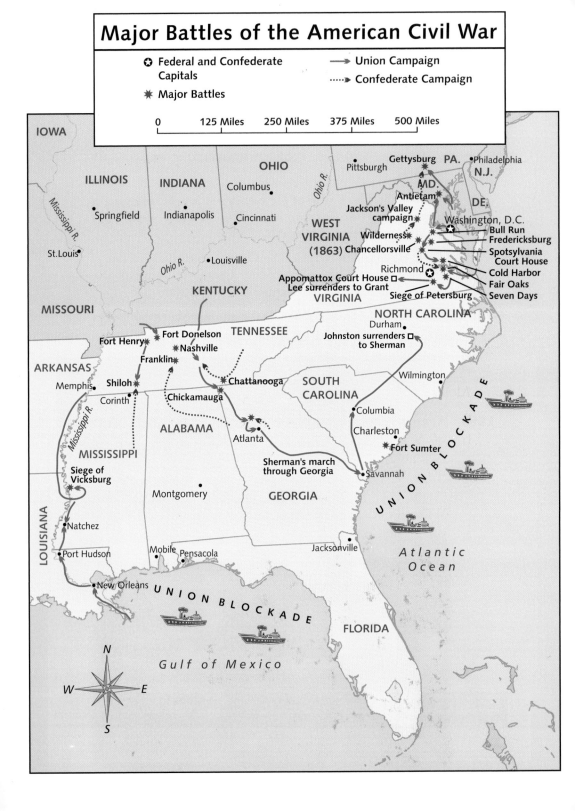

Major Battles of the American Civil War

Legend:
- ✪ Federal and Confederate Capitals
- ✳ Major Battles
- → Union Campaign
- ⇢ Confederate Campaign

Scale: 0 — 125 Miles — 250 Miles — 375 Miles — 500 Miles

IOWA

ILLINOIS

INDIANA

OHIO

Columbus

Springfield

Indianapolis

Cincinnati

St.Louis

Ohio R.

Louisville

WEST VIRGINIA (1863)

Pittsburgh

Gettysburg   PA.   •Philadelphia

N.J.

MD.

Antietam

Jackson's Valley campaign

Washington, D.C.

DE.

Bull Run

Wilderness   Fredericksburg

Chancellorsville   Spotsylvania Court House

Cold Harbor

Richmond

Appomattox Court House   Fair Oaks

Lee surrenders to Grant   Seven Days

VIRGINIA   Siege of Petersburg

MISSOURI

KENTUCKY

TENNESSEE

NORTH CAROLINA

Durham•

Johnston surrenders to Sherman

Fort Henry   Fort Donelson

Nashville

Franklin

Chattanooga

Wilmington

ARKANSAS

Memphis•   Shiloh

Corinth   Chickamauga

SOUTH CAROLINA

Columbia

Charleston

ALABAMA

Atlanta

Fort Sumter

MISSISSIPPI

Siege of Vicksburg

Montgomery

Sherman's march through Georgia

Savannah

GEORGIA

LOUISIANA

Natchez•

Port Hudson•

Mobile• Pensacola

Jacksonville•

Atlantic Ocean

New Orleans•   UNION BLOCKADE

FLORIDA

Gulf of Mexico

UNION BLOCKADE

N
W   E
S

Chapter 1

"A FEARFUL SHOCK": THREE PIVOTAL DAYS AT GETTYSBURG

The American Civil War began with clashes between Union and Confederate military forces in April 1861, only two months after the organization of the Confederate States of America in Montgomery, Alabama. Union and Confederate armies fought dozens of battles during the next four years until the Confederacy collapsed in the spring of 1865.

Until July 1863, Southern forces generally fared better than Northern armies, mostly because of the Confederacy's superior military leadership.

Robert E. Lee's decision to invade the North in July 1863 proved to be a turning point in the American Civil War.

But after 1863, as Confederate general Robert E. Lee said, the "overwhelming numbers and resources" of the Union army tipped the balance in the Union's favor.[1] And after the three-day Battle of Gettysburg, fought on the fields and hills of a small Pennsylvania town from July 1 to 3, 1863, the Confederacy remained on the defensive. It was never again able to mount an invasion of Northern territory.

▶ The Gettysburg Campaign

General Robert E. Lee, Confederate commander of the Army of Northern Virginia, decided to invade the North shortly after the Battle of Chancellorsville in May 1863. In that battle, Lee, outnumbered and undersupplied, had scored a smashing victory over General Joseph Hooker and the Army of the Potomac. But, with nearly thirteen thousand Confederate casualties, the Battle of Chancellorsville had been costly for Lee—and the greatest loss was that of his most competent corps commander, General T. J. "Stonewall" Jackson. Jackson was accidentally shot by Confederate soldiers while scouting the Union position. Despite these losses, Lee decided that Virginia and its people needed relief from the stress of battle, and his army desperately needed supplies, which were available in Pennsylvania.

Lee's army crossed Maryland and entered central Pennsylvania in June. Hooker, still in command of the Army of the Potomac, kept his army inside a semi-circle, always between Lee's army and the nation's capital in Washington, D.C.

▲ *General George G. Meade (seated, center) took over the Army of the Potomac less than a week before the Battle of Gettysburg.*

One of those who served under Hooker was Francis Adams Donaldson. Donaldson was born in Philadelphia on June 7, 1840. In 1858, he moved to Charleston, now in West Virginia but until 1863 still part of Virginia. When war broke out, his brother John joined the Confederate army, but Francis joined a Pennsylvania regiment. Captain Donaldson would go on to see action in all the major battles of the Army of the Potomac and survive, dying in 1928. But a week before the Battle of Gettysburg began, he expressed concern about his army's leadership.

Captain Donaldson reported on the Union army's activities on June 25:

> I don't know how long we will remain in this camp, but not for very long, as I presume both Lee and Hooker are manoeuvering for position. For the first time in a long while, the army critic is "dead beat," nothing to say, no suggestions to make—bewildered. . . . You can readily understand how completely at a loss we are to figure out the campaign and the object of our protracted stay at this point. I am in good health, and like all the rest of the brigade, in fine spirits, lacking only one thing to make us comfortable, and that is— faith in Hooker. We don't believe in him some how.[2]

After Chancellorsville, President Abraham Lincoln had also lost confidence in Hooker, so on June 28, he assigned General George Gordon Meade to command the Army of the Potomac. Lee continued northward, capturing Chambersburg and Carlisle, and finally, on July 1, arrived just northwest of Gettysburg. The town was a small but important crossroads where Lee's men could get supplies, especially shoes, which were badly needed by the Confederate troops.

Major Jedediah Hotchkiss, a mapmaker for the Confederate army, described their approach to Gettysburg on July 1:

> We marched towards Cashtown until we reached Middletown, having heard that the enemy was at Gettysburg. At Middletown we heard that A. P. Hill was approaching Gettysburg, from the mountains, so we turned with Rodes' Division and went on by the Middletown and

Gettysburg road until within some 2 miles of Gettysburg . . . We pressed forward and soon engaged the enemy on the hills to the west of Gettysburg. A. P. Hill attacked on our right about the same time. . . . We supped and [slept] just in the edge of the town. We killed and wounded large numbers of the enemy and took several thousand prisoners.[3]

The Battle: The First Day

On the afternoon of July 1, 1863, only a small number of Union cavalry, soldiers on horseback, defended Gettysburg. They were commanded by General John Buford. Units commanded by General Henry Heth, part of General Richard S. Ewell's Second Corps of the Confederate army, approached the town.

Most historians agree that Heth likely should have overrun Gettysburg that afternoon before Union reinforcements arrived, but he could not do so because of Union resistance from units led by Generals John Buford and John Reynolds. Their leadership gave Meade a chance to concentrate his force at Gettysburg to stop Lee's second and last invasion of the North. Joseph Rosengarten, a major in the Army of the Potomac, wrote about what had been accomplished that first day by the Union commanders.

Confederate topographer Jedediah Hotchkiss.

The brilliant achievement of Buford . . . is but too little considered in the history of the battle of Gettysburg. It was his
foresight and energy, his pluck and self-reliance, in thrust-
ing forward his forces and pushing the enemy, and thus
inviting, almost compelling their return, that brought on the
engagement of the first of July. Buford counted on Reynolds'
support, and he had it fully, faithfully, and energetically.[4]

But Buford would not have his support for long.
Reynolds, a native of Pennsylvania, had turned in his
saddle to see what troops were following when a bullet
struck him in the head. He died on the battle's first day.
His death was one of more than fifty thousand over the
three days at Gettysburg.

A Teacher Turns Nurse

The citizens living in Gettysburg were not spared the
effects of the battle. One Gettysburg native, a twenty-
one-year-old teacher named Elizabeth Salome "Sallie"
Myers, was on summer vacation in July 1863 when her
town became a battlefield. She later wrote about her
experiences from July 1 to 3.

On Wednesday July 1, the storm broke. We were brimming
over with patriotic enthusiasm. While our elders prepared
food we girls stood on the corner near our house and gave
refreshments of all kinds to "our boys" of the First Corps,
who were double-quicking down Washington Street to join
the troops already engaged in battle west of the town. After
the men had all passed, we sat on our doorsteps or stood
around in groups, frightened nearly out of our wits but

HERE IS THE PLACE.
WHERE GEN. REYNOLDS
WAS KILLED. JULY 1. 1863

The sign on this tree marks it as the place near the McPherson farm where General John Reynolds was mortally wounded during the first day of battle at Gettysburg. It was erected in the 1880s.

never dreaming of defeat. A horse was led by, the blood streaming from his head which was covered. The sight sickened me. Then a man was led by supported by two comrades. His head had been hastily bandaged and blood was visible. I turned away faint with horror, for I never could bear the sight of blood.[5]

But Sallie Myers overcame her fear to help care for the wounded and dying Union soldiers brought to Gettysburg homes and churches from the battlefield.

They had begun bringing wounded and injured into town. The Catholic and Presbyterian churches, a few doors east of

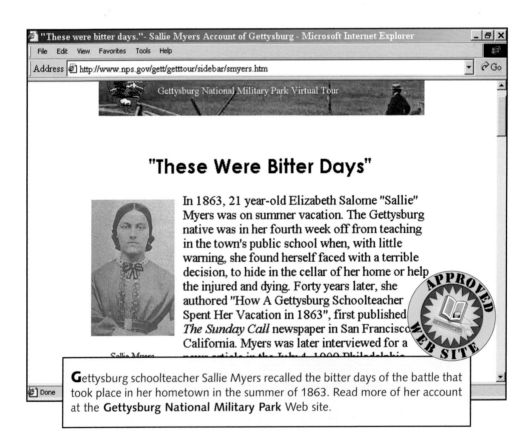

"These were bitter days."- Sallie Myers Account of Gettysburg - Microsoft Internet Explorer

File   Edit   View   Favorites   Tools   Help

Address http://www.nps.gov/gett/getttour/sidebar/smyers.htm

Gettysburg National Military Park Virtual Tour

"These Were Bitter Days"

In 1863, 21 year-old Elizabeth Salome "Sallie" Myers was on summer vacation. The Gettysburg native was in her fourth week off from teaching in the town's public school when, with little warning, she found herself faced with a terrible decision, to hide in the cellar of her home or help the injured and dying. Forty years later, she authored "How A Gettysburg Schoolteacher Spent Her Vacation in 1863", first published The Sunday Call newspaper in San Francisco California. Myers was later interviewed for a

Sallie Myers

Gettysburg schoolteacher Sallie Myers recalled the bitter days of the battle that took place in her hometown in the summer of 1863. Read more of her account at the **Gettysburg National Military Park** Web site.

my father's home were taken possesion of as hospitals. . . .
I went to the Catholic church. On pews and floors men lay,
the groans of the suffering and dying were heartrending. I
knelt beside the first man near the door and asked what I
could do. "Nothing," he replied, "I am going to die." I went
outside the church and cried. I returned and spoke to the
man—he was wounded in the lungs and spine, and there
was not the slightest hope for him. The man was Sgt.
Alexander Stewart of the 149th Pennsylvania Volunteers. I
read a chapter of the Bible to him, it was the last chapter his
father had read before he left home. The wounded man died
on Monday, July 6.

Sgt. Stewart was the first wounded man brought in, but
others followed. The sight of blood never again affected me
and I was among wounded and dying men day and night.[6]

The Second Day

Confederate soldiers, filing in from the west, occupied a
north-south line known as Seminary Ridge, and Union
forces did the same a mile or so to the east across an
open plain on Cemetery Ridge. Culp's Hill on the north
end and Big Round Top and Little Round Top on the
south, hills located on the Union side of the battlefield,
gave the area the appearance of a fishhook.

Lee planned to attack the Union line from his right
flank, or extreme southern end of the line, by late morning on July 2. But General James Longstreet, commander
in charge of the assault, believed that Confederate
forces should remain entrenched and let the Union army
attack them.

Lee decided that his army, as the invading force,
should begin the battle, but the attack did not come until

the afternoon. By then, Union soldiers in the 20th Maine Regiment were called in as reinforcements and, despite heavy losses, were able to hold the high ground at Little Round Top. Private Theodore Gerrish of the 20th Maine described the action:

> The rebels were confounded [confused]. . . . We struck them with a fearful shock. They recoil, stagger, break and run, and like avenging demons our men pursue. The rebels rush toward a stone wall, but, to our mutual surprise, two scores of rifle barrels gleam over the rocks, and a murderous volley was poured in upon them at close quarters.[7]

▶ The Third Day

On July 3, Lee planned another attack from the center of the line. General George E. Pickett's division led the charge, once again later than Lee had planned, because of Longstreet's delays. Pickett's men reached the Union line on Cemetery Ridge but could not break through. The Confederate assault was led by General Lewis Armistead, and Longstreet described his approach to the Union line:

> General Armistead, of the second line, spread his steps to supply the places of fallen comrades. His colors cut down, with a volley against the bristling line of bayonets, he put his cap on his sword to guide the storm. The enemy's massing, enveloping numbers held the struggle until the noble Armistead fell beside the wheels of the enemy's battery. . . .
>
> General Pickett, finding the battle broken while the enemy was still reinforcing, called the troops off.[8]

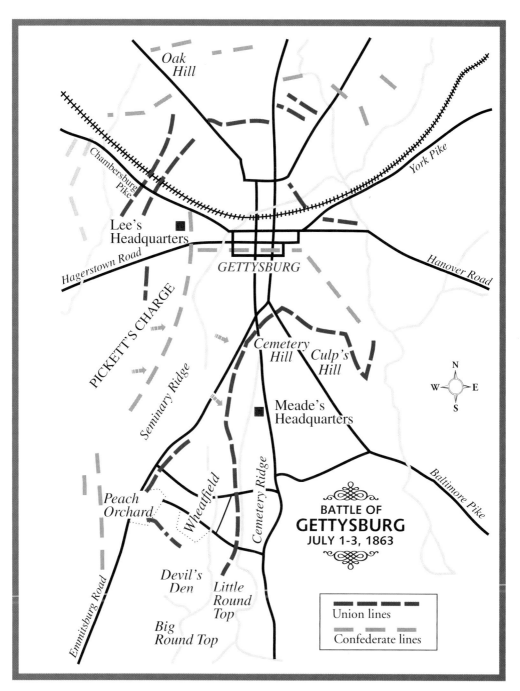

Oak
Hill

Chambersburg
Pike

York Pike

Lee's
Headquarters

Hagerstown Road

GETTYSBURG

Hanover Road

PICKETT'S CHARGE

Seminary Ridge

Cemetery
Hill

Culp's
Hill

N
W — E
S

Meade's
Headquarters

Peach
Orchard

Wheatfield

Cemetery Ridge

Baltimore Pike

BATTLE OF
GETTYSBURG
JULY 1-3, 1863

Emmitsburg Road

Devil's
Den

Little
Round
Top

Big
Round Top

Union lines
Confederate lines

▲ In this map of the battlefield at Gettysburg, the Confederate forces can be
seen to the north, while the Union forces were south of the town.

▷ Defeat and Retreat

More than half of the Confederates who had charged the Union line on that third day were killed, and some Confederate units were completely destroyed. When the Battle of Gettysburg was over, the Confederate army had suffered twenty-eight thousand casualties; the Union army, twenty-three thousand. When only a few survivors straggled back to Seminary Ridge, Lee knew he must return to Virginia. Jedediah Hotchkiss reported that Lee had him up at 2:00 A.M. on July 4 working on a map for the army to use on its retreat to Virginia:

> Major Harman, the Chief Q.M. [quartermaster, the officer responsible for feeding and clothing the troops] of the 2nd. Corps, started, about 3 A.M., with a train of baggage and captured property for Williamsport. The General [Ewell] told him to get the train safely across the Potomac or he wanted to see his face no more. . . . Our loss was very heavy yesterday.[9]

Lee's invasion of Pennsylvania in the summer of 1863 has been called "the high tide" of the Confederacy. After the Battle of Gettysburg, the tide turned in favor of the Union. Confederate armies never again mounted an invasion of the North. They could only hope to defend their own territory and outlast Northern resolve to compel their return to the Union. Time finally ran out for the Confederacy in the spring of 1865, but the Union victory at Gettysburg in the summer of 1863 marked a turning point in America's Civil War.

A HOUSE DIVIDED: A BRIEF HISTORY OF THE CIVIL WAR

Tensions between citizens of Northern and Southern states over states' rights and slavery developed in the United States early in the nation's history. Congress settled the issue of slavery's expansion in the area of the Louisiana Purchase in 1820 by agreeing to admit Missouri as a slave state (one where slavery was legal) and Maine as a "free" state (one where slavery was prohibited by

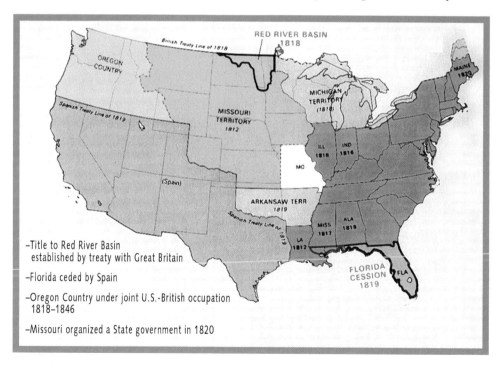

–Title to Red River Basin
  established by treaty with Great Britain

–Florida ceded by Spain

–Oregon Country under joint U.S.-British occupation
  1818–1846

–Missouri organized a State government in 1820

▲ *The question of slavery's expansion was settled, for a time, in 1820 with the admission of Missouri as a slave state and Maine as a free state. This map shows the United States in that year.*

law). Legislation also barred slavery above 36 degrees, 30 minutes north latitude, in the purchase area.

Then, after this Missouri Compromise, almost every issue discussed by Congress during the next four decades involved slavery in one way or another. Delays in the admission of Texas to the Union and how territory won from Mexico in a war fought from 1846 to 1848 should be developed are examples of issues in the national political debate dominated by slavery.[1]

▷ Wedges of Separation

In the decade or so before the Civil War, a series of sharp divisions between slave states and non-slave states occurred. Historian J. G. Randall called these divisions "wedges of separation." Randall likened these disagreements to wedges, or tools, used to split fence rails. None alone could achieve that goal, but the growing impact of the successive wedges could split the largest and toughest log. The following events, then, could be thought of as wedges that eventually split the Union, produced secession of the Southern, or slave, states, and resulted in civil war.

First, the national Methodist and Baptist churches divided in 1845 and 1846 over the issue of slavery. Most Northern church members believed slavery was morally wrong, but Southern members thought of slavery as a political and economic right, and neither side wished to continue to worship in the same denomination. This led to the development of Northern and Southern organizations in both denominations. Other churches also felt such strains, although not all of them formed separate organizations.

The question of admitting California to the Union also divided the nation. California wished to enter the Union as a free state, but Southern congressmen feared that this would upset the balance in the United States Senate between slave states and free states, a situation that would compel Southern states to secede.

The Compromise of 1850, then, admitted California as a free state but organized Utah and New Mexico territories without reference to slavery. It also barred the

These slaves from Virginia were photographed in 1862. Slavery had divided the nation long before the first shots were fired at Fort Sumter.

slave trade in Washington, D.C., and enacted a fugitive slave law, which gave federal law enforcement the authority to help Southerners reclaim slaves who had escaped to free states.

Those who demanded an immediate end to slavery were known as abolitionists. Their constant demands for the end of slavery kept tensions high between Northerners and Southerners throughout the 1850s. An excellent example of abolitionist influence was the publication in 1852 of Harriet Beecher Stowe's novel *Uncle Tom's Cabin*. The book, an attack on slavery, quickly became a best seller. Northerners generally accepted its portrayal of slavery as true, but most Southerners regarded the same information as false.

Even the attempts to build a transcontinental railroad, a rail line across the continent to the Pacific Coast, were affected by slavery because people believed that if the railroad moved westward from an area where slavery was allowed, then slavery would be more likely to expand westward, too.[2]

The Election of 1860 and Secession

Selecting the president of the United States in 1860 became the final "wedge of separation." Southerners vowed that the election of any Republican as president would force them to secede, or leave the Union, because the Republican party's platform (declaration of its principles) called for the end of slavery.

When Republican Abraham Lincoln defeated Democrats Stephen A. Douglas and John C. Breckinridge and

Constitutional Union party candidate John Bell, delegates to a secession convention in South Carolina decided that their state should leave the Union.

Soon, Mississippi, Alabama, Florida, Georgia, and Louisiana also voted to secede. Only Texas among the Gulf States hesitated because its governor, Sam Houston, was a Unionist. Within a month, secessionists in Texas overwhelmed Houston's opposition to secession.[3]

Writing a Constitution for the CSA

All seven states that had seceded by February 1861 sent delegates to Montgomery, Alabama, to organize the Confederate States of America. The delegates hurried their work so they could have their new government up and running before the inauguration of President Lincoln on March 4, 1861.

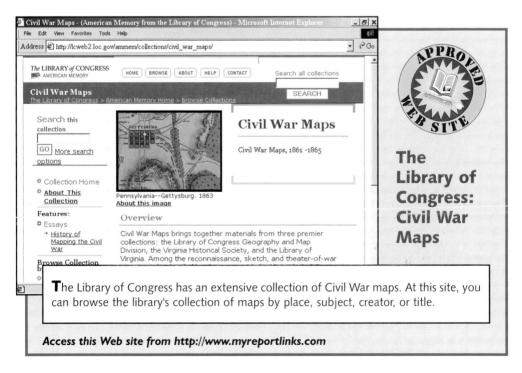

The Library of Congress has an extensive collection of Civil War maps. At this site, you can browse the library's collection of maps by place, subject, creator, or title.

Access this Web site from http://www.myreportlinks.com

Delegates to the convention in Montgomery produced a constitution for the new Confederacy that was remarkably similar to the Constitution of the United States. This was not surprising, because Southerners supported the United States Constitution. They also believed, however,

▲ Jefferson Davis's inauguration as president of the Confederate States of America was held in Richmond, Virginia, the Confederacy's capital, on February 22, 1862.

that Northern political leaders had not interpreted or enforced it properly.

The Confederate constitution called for a government of executive, legislative, and judicial branches, just as the United States Constitution did. However, the Confederate president would serve a term of six years and not be eligible to serve two consecutive terms.[4]

Organizing the Government of the Confederacy

Delegates to the convention in Montgomery selected Jefferson F. Davis of Mississippi as provisional president and Alexander H. Stephens of Georgia as provisional vice president. Confederate voters later confirmed both choices in an election.

Davis had been born in Kentucky but moved to Mississippi with his family while still young. He graduated from the United States Military Academy at West Point and was a hero of the Mexican-American War. Davis served as governor of Mississippi and was a United States senator when Mississippi seceded.[5]

President Davis organized a cabinet to run executive departments, taking care that each of the other six Confederate states was represented. Davis assumed that he represented Mississippi in the government. Over the four-year existence of the Confederacy, only Texan John H. Reagan, who served as postmaster general, and Stephen Mallory of Florida, who served as secretary of the Navy, held their jobs the entire time. Six men served as secretary of war, and one, Judah P. Benjamin of

Louisiana, held three cabinet posts—attorney general, secretary of war, and secretary of state.

▶ Enlarging the Confederacy

Seceding states, and then the Confederate government, demanded that the United States surrender all federal property located within their borders.

While all states made such demands, South Carolina's insistence that the Union surrender Fort Sumter, located on an island in Charleston Harbor, became the most significant dispute. Major Robert Anderson, a Kentuckian by birth, commanded the fort, and he insisted that he could

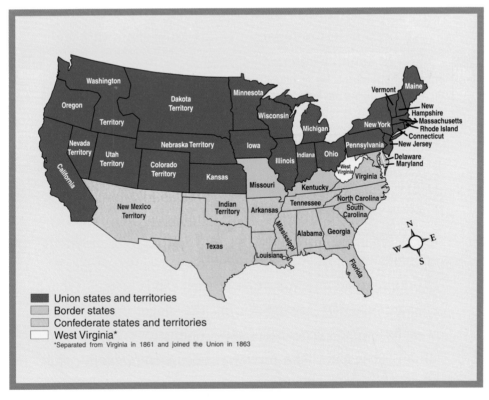

Union states and territories
Border states
Confederate states and territories
West Virginia*
*Separated from Virginia in 1861 and joined the Union in 1863

▲ A map of the United States at the time of the Civil War shows the country divided into Union states and territories, Confederate states and territories, border states, and West Virginia, which entered the Union in 1863.

not surrender as long as he had supplies, but suggested that he would surrender when he could no longer feed his men and provide them with arms and ammunition. But Confederate general P.G.T. Beauregard grew impatient with the delay, so on April 12, Southern forces opened fire on the fort, and Anderson agreed to surrender after he and his men were bombarded for a day.

President Lincoln, who determined to hold the Union together, called for seventy-five thousand volunteers for military service to deal with the rebellion in South Carolina. His request, which went to all states in the Union, caused the citizens of Arkansas, Tennessee, Virginia, and North Carolina to secede from the Union and then join the Confederacy. They refused to make war on other Southerners.[6]

Citizens in Missouri, Kentucky, Delaware, and Maryland, the only other states that permitted slavery, also considered secession, but did not secede. These "border states," located between the Confederacy and the remainder of the Union, claimed many citizens who did not approve of slavery or believe secession legal or justified. When fighting in the Civil War began, much of it occurred in these border states and Virginia.

Dissent in the Confederacy

Not all of those who lived in the South supported slavery or secession, and their dissent caused many problems for the Confederate government.

Virginia suffered most from internal dissent. Mountain-area residents who lived in western Virginia owned few slaves and did not share the attitudes of Tidewater, or eastern, Virginians about secession. When the eastern majority voted for Virginia to secede from the Union on April 17, 1861, western Virginians began planning their own separation from their state. By 1863, these dissenters had established the state of West Virginia, and the United States Congress accepted them into the Union. Thus Virginia, site of the Confederate capital in Richmond, lost approximately 40 percent of its land area and population. Serious opposition to secession also developed in eastern Tennessee but did not lead to a similar separation within the state.[7]

Newspaper editors Robert Barnwell Rhett of the *Charleston Mercury* and Edward A. Pollard of the *Richmond Examiner* severely criticized President Davis and other Confederate officials for every setback in the Confederate war for independence.

Issues such as impressments, or the seizure of private property—everything from livestock feed to fence rails for fuel for soldier's campfires—offended many Confederate citizens. Conscription, or compulsory military service, also irritated Southerners, especially those who did not want to serve and those

◁ *The president of the Confederacy, Jefferson Davis, like his Union counterpart Abraham Lincoln, was born in Kentucky.*

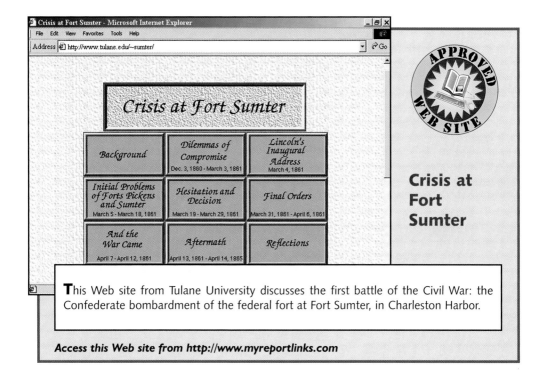

Crisis at Fort Sumter - Microsoft Internet Explorer

File   Edit   View   Favorites   Tools   Help

Address ⓔ http://www.tulane.edu/~sumter/   ▼ ⏣ Go

Crisis at Fort Sumter

Background	Dilemmas of Compromise Dec. 3, 1860 - March 3, 1861	Lincoln's Inaugural Address March 4, 1861
Initial Problems of Forts Pickens and Sumter March 5 - March 18, 1861	Hesitation and Decision March 19 - March 29, 1861	Final Orders March 31, 1861 - April 6, 1861
And the War Came April 7 - April 12, 1861	Aftermath April 13, 1861 - April 14, 1865	Reflections

Crisis at Fort Sumter

This Web site from Tulane University discusses the first battle of the Civil War: the Confederate bombardment of the federal fort at Fort Sumter, in Charleston Harbor.

Access this Web site from http://www.myreportlinks.com

who already had volunteered and did not trust soldiers who were forced to enter the army.

Some Southerners opposed measures of the central Confederate government because of long-held views on states' rights, or the belief that the authority of the state was superior to the authority of the central government in some matters.

▶ Confederate Economy

It would be inaccurate to think of the Confederacy as a vast plantation or farm, because the South did have limited industrial development. But it is true that America's southland was heavily agricultural before and during the Civil War.

Cotton growing dominated in the Gulf South states, or South Carolina westward to Texas, with sugarcane the most widespread crop in the lower portions of Louisiana. The Upper South, mainly North Carolina, Virginia, and Tennessee, produced large crops of tobacco, corn, and grains. Despite heavy concentration on these "cash crops" grown for market, growers in all Confederate states also produced food crops for their own use.

Lacking the Machinery of War

In contrast to such heavy investment in agriculture, the Confederacy contained less industry. A few textile mills, or factories where fiber was converted to thread and woven into cloth, operated in North Carolina. Only the Tredegar Iron Works, located in Richmond, had a large enough foundry to produce both railroad locomotives and cannon.

With the coming of war, Tredegar's operators were required to concentrate on making cannons, which meant that damaged or worn-out locomotives could not be replaced. This weakened the Confederate transportation system and ultimately the war effort itself. By 1865, some Southerners were starving while food rotted in faraway fields because it could not be transported to market.

One bright spot in Confederate industry was the work of its Ordnance Bureau, headed by Josiah Gorgas. Gorgas worked miracles to provide Confederate soldiers with weapons and ammunition. To his credit, no battle loss could be attributed to a lack of these essential fighting tools.[8]

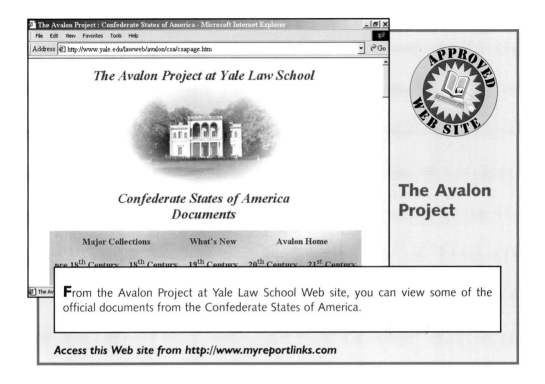

The Avalon Project at Yale Law School

Confederate States of America
Documents

Major Collections   What's New   Avalon Home

pre 18th Century   18th Century   19th Century   20th Century   21st Century

The Avalon Project

From the Avalon Project at Yale Law School Web site, you can view some of the official documents from the Confederate States of America.

Access this Web site from http://www.myreportlinks.com

▶ Confederate Finance

At the beginning of the Civil War, the government of the Confederacy had to establish taxes, create new currency (paper money), and establish a new national economy.

There were many reasons why the Confederacy's financial situation was difficult. The city of New Orleans, the South's largest banking center, fell under Union occupation in April 1862, during the first year of the war. This deprived the Confederacy of vital financial resources and experience.

Confederate congressmen first attempted to raise needed revenue by asking Southern state legislatures to provide money. Later, they resorted to an income tax and a tax-in-kind, a tax in which citizens paid their taxes with what they produced—food, cotton, horses, and so on.

Confederate congressmen also authorized their treasury department to issue large amounts of currency that they asked the citizens of the Confederate states to accept at face value—money not backed by gold or silver coins. Such bills were actually promissory notes. This meant that the government promised to pay the person who had the bill its value in gold at a future date. Such money dropped in value when people lost confidence in the government's ability to keep its promise to pay them in gold.[9]

Sustaining the Union

Abraham Lincoln believed that the Union could not be dissolved by secession. He dedicated every effort to bringing the seceded states back into the Union.

Like Jefferson Davis, Abraham Lincoln was also born in Kentucky but later moved north with his family to Indiana and then Illinois. Lincoln became a lawyer and served a term in Congress during the 1840s but returned to his practice in Illinois when the sectional crisis of the Union heated up in the 1850s. He joined the new Republican party because it opposed slavery and became its presidential nominee in 1860. Lincoln defeated three other candidates in the national election on November 6 and was elected the sixteenth president of the United States. In his inaugural address, delivered on March 4, 1861, President Lincoln told the seceded states that he did not want war but that he would preserve the Union:

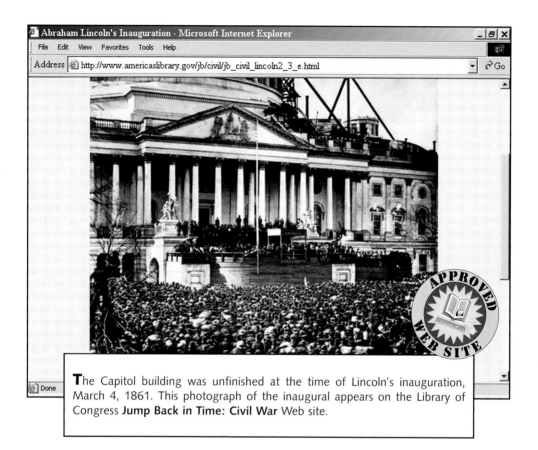

The Capitol building was unfinished at the time of Lincoln's inauguration, March 4, 1861. This photograph of the inaugural appears on the Library of Congress **Jump Back in Time: Civil War** Web site.

In *your* hands, my dissatisfied fellow countrymen, and not in *mine,* is the momentous issue of civil war. The government will not assail *you.* You can have no conflict without being yourselves the aggressors. *You* have no oath registered in Heaven to destroy the government, while *I* shall have the most solemn one to "preserve, protect, and defend it."

Lincoln offered friendship to the South in the final words of his address:

We are not enemies, but friends. We must not be enemies. Though passion may have strained, it must not break our bonds of affection. The mystic chords of memory, stretching from every battlefield and patriot grave, to every living heart and hearthstone, all over this broad land, will yet swell the chorus of the Union, when again touched, as surely they will be, by the better angels of our nature.[10]

President Lincoln was willing to do anything to preserve the Union. To isolate the Confederacy and prevent its government from trading with other countries, he

U.S. Civil War Effects on People: Primary Sources - Microsoft Internet Explorer

File   Edit   View   Favorites   Tools   Help

Address http://www.ket.org/civilwar/primary.html   Go

Primary Sources: Civil War Effects

The Civil War affected Kentuckians in many different ways. Here are some primary sources -- letters, diaries, and personal memoirs -- that offer us a picture of how several Kentuckians in various circumstances experienced those times.

Causes of the Civil War

ivided -- Many families were divided by the Civil War, as parents r brothers and sisters found themselves on opposite sides. The ters and diary entries give a few examples:

Kentucky Educational Television's **Primary Sources: Civil War Effects** contains diary accounts, letters, and personal memoirs from individuals and families from Kentucky whose lives were affected by the Civil War.

EDITOR'S CHOICE

proclaimed a blockade. United States Navy ships patrolled the Confederate coastline from Chesapeake Bay in Virginia to Brownsville, Texas, and by 1865, only one in ten ships attempting to run to blockade reached shore.

Expanding the Powers of the Presidency

When Confederates fired on Fort Sumter on April 12, 1861, President Lincoln declared South Carolina in rebellion and then greatly enlarged the voluntary army to suppress it.

Lincoln's administration arrested several thousand Americans for disloyalty, and he also pardoned a great many soldiers convicted of such things as falling asleep while on sentry duty. In doing all these things, Lincoln greatly expanded the powers of the presidency.

Dissent in the Union

Not everyone agreed with Lincoln's policy of forcing the seceded states to return to the Union. Some who lived in the North either believed that a state did have the power to secede or that the Union lacked legal authority to force states to remain in the Union. Others believed that slavery was a matter for the people of each state to decide for themselves.

When such people disagreed with government policy, it led them to obstruct the Union war effort, or support the Confederacy while living in the Union. They were called Copperheads after a snake whose body is colored like the floor of the forest but whose head is a distinctly different color. In other words, "Copperheads" lived in the Union but thought like Confederates.[11]

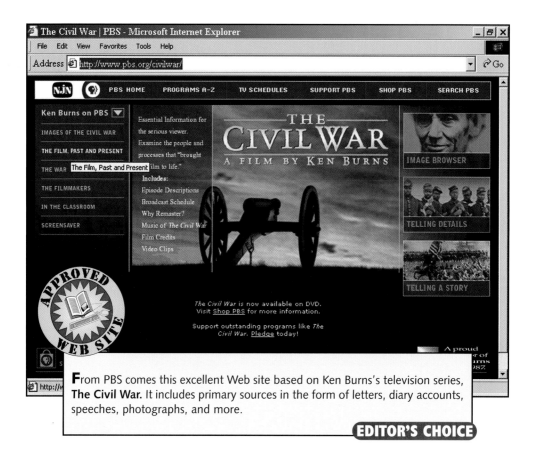

From PBS comes this excellent Web site based on Ken Burns's television series, **The Civil War.** It includes primary sources in the form of letters, diary accounts, speeches, photographs, and more.

EDITOR'S CHOICE

▷ The Economy of the Union

Just as the Confederacy was not one large agricultural plantation, the Union was not one giant factory. All Northern states had extensive agriculture, and even more important, most crops grown in the North were edible and therefore of more immediate use. But it is also true that most of America's manufacturing and heavy industries, including those that made iron, were located in the North. Most of the shoes, clothes, wagons, tools, and other items used daily came from the North. The industries of the Northern states gave the Union an advantage in the Civil War because the North could manufacture so much more of the necessities of war than the South could.

Financing the Union Effort

The Union paid the costs of making war by imposing taxes, by borrowing money, and by issuing paper currency. United States paper currency, known as "greenbacks" because of the color of ink used to print the bills, maintained its value much better than Confederate money because the Union was well established. And win or lose, people expected the Union to survive and meet its financial obligations.[12]

Raising Armies

In 1861, approximately sixteen thousand men served in the armed forces of the United States. By the war's end, according to the best estimates, more than 2 million men served in the United States military. Between 750,000 and 850,000 men served in the Confederate army.

Both sides ultimately had to resort to conscription, or the military draft, but in 1861, hundreds of thousands of soldiers volunteered for service in both armies. Whether in the North or South, usually a locally prominent leader would raise a company, which consisted of approximately one hundred men, and it would most likely be named for him.

Companies would be combined to form regiments, regiments into brigades, brigades into divisions, divisions into corps, and corps into armies. Captains commanded companies, and generals commanded armies, with majors and colonels commanding the units in between.

The war was not merely fought in one region by two opposing armies, however. There were three theaters, or areas, in which the fighting took place: the eastern theater, from the Atlantic Ocean to the Appalachian Mountains; the western theater, from the western side of the Appalachians to the Mississippi River; and the Trans-Mississippi West, which was made up of the territories and states of the far west.

Generally, the Union named its armies after bodies of water while the Confederacy named its armies after large geographic areas. So in the eastern theater of the war, the Army of the Potomac (Union), opposed the Army of Northern Virginia (Confederate). Sometimes they identified battles by different names for the same reason. So while the Union army was fighting the Battle of Bull Run on July 21, 1861, the Confederate army called that same combat the Battle of Manassas.[13]

How the Armies Fared

Few battles in the Civil War were really decisive. Usually armies clashed, then backed off, recovered, and clashed again weeks or months later, with the Union army in the east always trying to capture Richmond while the Confederates defended their capital.

Confederate commanders generally were more successful than Union commanders from 1861 until July 1864 because of better leadership and because they fought a defensive strategy. In other words, Confederates did not have to defeat the Union to win—they only had

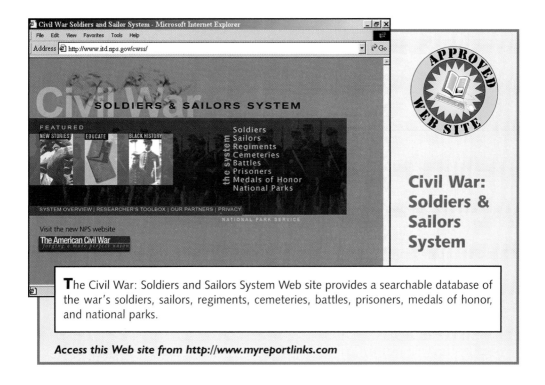

The Civil War: Soldiers and Sailors System Web site provides a searchable database of the war's soldiers, sailors, regiments, cemeteries, battles, prisoners, medals of honor, and national parks.

Access this Web site from http://www.myreportlinks.com

to survive, but the Union had to defeat the Confederacy to achieve its goal of reunion.

After nearly simultaneous Union victories at Gettysburg, Pennsylvania, on July 3, 1863, and the fall of Vicksburg, Mississippi, the next day, July 4, the greater strength of the Union army turned the tide in its favor.

Despite earlier Confederate victories in the east at Manassas, Fredericksburg, and Chancellorsville, and modest successes in the west at Shiloh, the Union army usually won the battles after 1863.

Finally, on April 9, 1865, Confederate general Robert E. Lee surrendered his Army of Northern Virginia to Union general Ulysses S. Grant at Appomattox Court

Hd. Qrs: Army of N. Va:
10 April 1865—

Genl Orders
No. 9

After four years of arduous service, marked by unsurpassed Courage & fortitude, the army of Northern Virginia has been Compelled to yield to overwhelming numbers & resources.

I need not tell the brave survivors of so many hard fought battles, who have remained steadfast to the last, that I have Consented to the result from no distrust of them; but feeling that valor & devotion Could accomplish nothing that would Compensate for the loss that must have attended the Continuance of the Contest; I determined to avoid the useless sacrifice of those, whose past services have endeared them to their Countrymen.

By the terms of the agreement, officers and men Can return to their homes & remain until exchanged. You will take with you the satisfaction that proceeds from the Consciousness of duty faithfully performed, and I earnestly pray that a Merciful God will extend to you His blessing & protection.

With an increasing admiration of your Constancy & devotion to your Country, & a grateful remembrance of your kind & generous Consideration for myself, I bid you all an affectionate farewell

R E Lee
Genl

General Lee's farewell letter to his troops in the Army of Northern Virginia spoke of his gratitude for their "service . . . marked by unsurpassed courage. . . ."

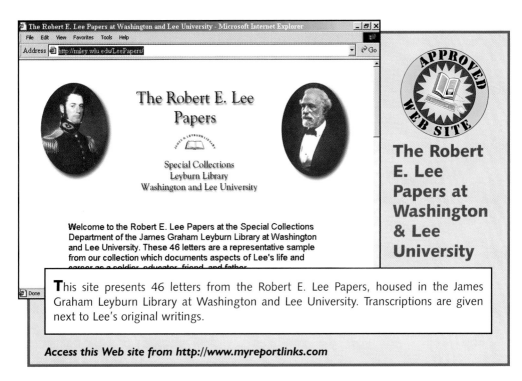

The Robert E. Lee Papers at Washington and Lee University - Microsoft Internet Explorer

File   Edit   View   Favorites   Tools   Help

Address | http://miley.wlu.edu/LeePapers/ | Go

The Robert E. Lee Papers

Special Collections
Leyburn Library
Washington and Lee University

Welcome to the Robert E. Lee Papers at the Special Collections
Department of the James Graham Leyburn Library at Washington
and Lee University. These 46 letters are a representative sample
from our collection which documents aspects of Lee's life and

The Robert E. Lee Papers at Washington & Lee University

This site presents 46 letters from the Robert E. Lee Papers, housed in the James Graham Leyburn Library at Washington and Lee University. Transcriptions are given next to Lee's original writings.

Access this Web site from http://www.myreportlinks.com

House, Virginia. Ten days later, Confederate general
J. E. Johnston surrendered the Army of Tennessee to
Union general William T. Sherman. Robert E. Lee bid his
army farewell with the following words:

> After four years of arduous service marked by unsurpassed
> courage and fortitude, the Army of Northern Virginia has
> been compelled to yield to overwhelming numbers and
> resources. I need not tell the survivors of so many hard-
> fought battles, who have remained steadfast to the last,
> that I have consented to this result from no distrust of them;
> but, feeling that valor and devotion could accomplish noth-
> ing that could compensate for the loss that would have
> attended the continuation of the contest, I have determined
> to avoid the useless sacrifice of those whose past services
> have endeared them to their countrymen.[14]

Chapter 3 ▶

IN THE WORDS OF UNION SOLDIERS

Fewer than twenty thousand men served in the United States Army on the eve of the Civil War. About half of them occupied posts on a north-south frontier line that stretched from Wisconsin to Texas.

In April 1861, President Abraham Lincoln enlarged the United States Army by summoning seventy-five thousand volunteer soldiers to deal with the rebellion in South Carolina. As the war expanded, many more volunteered for service. After 1863, others were drafted into service. Eventually, more than one million men wore the blue uniform of the Union army during the Civil War.

These new soldiers expected to serve until the war ended, then return to civilian jobs and activities. They volunteered eagerly to preserve the Union, but eventually they also accepted ending slavery as a primary goal of the war as it progressed.[1]

When soldiers left home during the Civil War, writing and receiving letters was their only way to share their experiences as soldiers and learn of the welfare of loved ones and friends. A great many of those letters have been preserved by descendants or are held in archives, and many have been published. Soldiers' letters and diary entries offer us a firsthand look at what life was like for those who fought in the American Civil War.

By the President of the United States of America:

A Proclamation.

Whereas, on the twenty-second day of September, in the year of our Lord one thousand eight hundred and sixty-two, a proclamation was issued by the President of the United States, containing, among other things, the following, to wit:

"That on the first day of January, in the

Featured Documents

NATIONAL ARCHIVES & RECORDS ADMINISTRATION

PRINT-FRIENDLY VERSION

Exhibit Hall

Treaty of Kanagawa

Whistler's Survey Etching

The D.C. Emancipation Act

▶ The Emancipation Proclamation

Henry O. Flipper

The 19th Amendment

German Surrender Document

Japanese Surrender Document

The Marshall Plan

The North Atlantic Treaty

Jackie Robinson's Letter

Friendship 7 Transcript

Apollo 1

The Emancipation Proclamation

President Abraham Lincoln issued the Emancipation Proclamation on January 1, 1863, as the nation approached its third year of bloody civil war. The proclamation declared "that all persons held as slaves" within the rebellious states "are, and henceforward shall be free."

Despite this expansive wording, the Emancipation Proclamation was limited in many ways. It applied only to states that had seceded from the Union, leaving slavery untouched in the loyal border states. It also expressly exempted parts of the Confederacy that had already come under Northern control. Most important, the freedom it promised depended upon Union military victory.

Although the Emancipation Proclamation did not immediately free a single slave, it fundamentally transformed the character of the war. After January 1, 1863, every advance of federal troops expanded the domain of freedom. Moreover, the Proclamation announced the acceptance of black men into the Union Army and Navy, enabling the liberated to become liberators. By the

APPROVED
WEB SITE

Featured Documents: The Emancipation Proclamation

This National Archives Web site contains images and transcriptions of Abraham Lincoln's drafts and final version of the Emancipation Proclamation, pictured above, which went into effect in January 1863.

Access this Web site from http://www.myreportlinks.com

▶ Joining the Army

Men joined the Union army for a variety of reasons, but noble ideas such as patriotism and preserving the Union were high on the list.

Charles W. Gould responded to President Lincoln's call for volunteers on June 5, 1861. He was the first of seven brothers to volunteer for the war, enlisting at a recruiting station on Staten Island, New York. He was placed in Company I, 3rd Regiment of the New York Excelsior Brigade. On June 9, Charles Gould wrote of early camp experiences in a letter to his sister, Hannah Gould Thomas:

> Embracing the first opportunity I write to inform you that I am well & in good spirits after leaving home. I went to Hancock [New York], joined the Delhi company Tuesday night, got on the cars about 2 oclock wensday morning, ate breakfast in New York at 11 oclock & came immeditly to staten's island. . . . It is very hot & the excitement is intence. . . .The first night I sleep under some thick cloth with an oil cloth under me and with the others cathed [catched] a heavy cold but am well now.[2]

Gould told his sister about having crackers with some beef and coffee for breakfast. His companions, he said, were "of the roughest kind, gambling fighting & swearing seem to be the principal amusement, little thinking that a vast number of them will never see home again."[3]

Gould himself never saw home again. Like so many young men who perished in the Civil War, his death was the result of disease rather than combat. Charles Gould died of typhoid fever at Camp Wool, Staten Island, on February 11, 1862, which was just nine months after he had enlisted. He was twenty years old.

Fighting for His Own Freedom: The African-American Soldier

Abolitionist and former slave Frederick Douglass advocated the use of black soldiers in the Union army as soon as the war began. But it was not until 1863 that President Lincoln permitted them to serve. Even so, they could only serve in units that were segregated and could not receive commissions. Approximately three hundred thousand African Americans eventually served in the Union army during the war, and Douglass was instrumental in recruiting many of them. Among those he recruited were his own sons Charles and Lewis. They both enlisted in the 54th Massachusetts Regiment although Charles later moved to a cavalry division.

On July 6, 1863, Charles Douglass wrote to his father from Camp Meigs in Massachusetts, where he had just returned after spending two days in Boston. In it, he hails the recent Union victory at Gettysburg and tells of an incident with a white man of Irish heritage. Douglass, like other black soldiers, encountered racism even though they were willing to fight and die for the Union.

> This morning as I was about to take the train for camp I saw some returned soldiers from Newbern, N.C. We had just got the news that Meade had whipped the Rebels [referring to the victory at Gettysburg] and behind me stood a[n] Irishman. I said that we had some sort of a Gen. now [in

praise of Meade] and that made the Irish[man] mad and he stepped in front of me with his fist doubled up in my face and said, "ain't McClellan a good Gen [referring to the general who had once commanded the Army of the Potomac] . . . I don't care if you have got the uniform on." When he got done I was so mad that I sweat freely and I drew my coat and went at him. All the time there was a policeman on the opposite side watching our movements. Just as I went "at" him (he was heavier than me) the policeman came and stopped me and asked what the matter was. I told him and he marched the other fellow off and that made all the other Irish mad and I felt better still. I felt as though I could whip a dozen Irish.[4]

Charles Douglass, pictured, and his brother Lewis were two of more than 300,000 African Americans who fought for the Union. Learn more about them and their famous father at **American Visionaries: Frederick Douglass,** the Web site for Cedar Hill, the Douglass home, now preserved through the National Park Service.

▶ Facing Combat

Many soldiers expected that the war would not last long, perhaps even be concluded by a single decisive battle. But such a battle did not occur, and the war dragged on.

John Pardington had enlisted as a private in Captain Isaac Ingersoll's Company B, Twenty-fourth Michigan Volunteers, part of the famous Iron Brigade. He wrote his wife, Sarah, on September 2, 1862, about campaign life:

It is in Haste I write these few lines to you for we are now under marching orders either to Bull Run or back to Washington. The enemys cavalry are now in full force a few miles from us. . . . Dear we are all in good spirits and well. We arrived here last night and just as we got here it comes on a heavy rain storm. Not a tent to cover us but I soon found out a old shed just about like Joes old cow shed and I slept good till morning although wet through. . . . Dear Sarah I dont think it will be long before we are ordered to the Battle feild.[5]

The next day, Pardington revealed in another letter how anxious he was about combat:

Dear Wife
Kiss the Baby for me and Write as soon as you get this and tell me the news at home for when I write again I suppose I shall tell you if I am spared how being on a battle feels. Remember me to all and a Kiss for the Baby and except [accept] one for yourself. So good By God Bless you and give me your Prayers.[6]

Like John Pardington, this young soldier, also a private, served in a Michigan unit.

Private Pardington was not spared "how being on a battle feels." He was killed on July 1, 1863, in the first day of fighting at Gettysburg.

▶ Women Soldiers

The letters written to Hannah Gould Thomas and Sarah Pardington show not only what was happening to their loved ones in service, but also provide examples of how most Union women lived during the Civil War. They supported sons, brothers, and husbands who served in the army while they remained at home caring for farms, families, and businesses. There were other women, such as nurses, who became more directly involved in the war, and even quite a few women who disguised themselves as men to join the fighting. One of those was Sarah Rosetta Wakeman.

Sarah Rosetta Wakeman, or Private Lyons Wakeman, dressed in men's clothing and enlisted in the 153rd Regiment, New York State Volunteers. Wakeman, who came from a large farm family in central New York State, left home for several reasons, among them a family disagreement. Knowing men made much more money than women, she first disguised her gender to get work on a riverboat, but when she found out that she could make more money in the service, she changed her mind. After all, life on the farm for the oldest child of nine had already taught her to do many of the chores that men did, and she was able to shoot a gun. Her letters home to her family explained her decision.

> When I got there i saw some soldiers. They wanted I should enlist and so i did. I got 100 and 52$ in money. I enlisted for 3 years or soon [as] discharged. All the money i send you i want you should spend it for the family in clothing or something to eat. . . . If i ever return i shall have money enough for my self and to divide with you.[7]

For some time, Wakeman's unit served on guard duty in Washington, D.C. In a letter written on September 3, 1863, Private Wakeman described life as a guard.

> I was on Camp guard yesterday and got relieve this morning at nine O'Clock. Our regiment have to guard five different

Manville Public Library
Manville, New Jersey

places. One is Camp guard, Second is Carroll prison, third is Depot guard, fourth is City hall, and the fifth is City guard. . . . The City Hall guard is where the draft is Carried on here. There they exam [ine] the men there and Some of them get exempt. They have drafted black men as well as White men. When the men is passed into the army, they are taken off by a guard to the place of rendezvous.[8]

In 1864, Wakeman served in General Nathaniel Banks's Red River Campaign in Louisiana. She, like other women, was able to pass as a man because no medical exams were required to enlist. But all women who disguised themselves as men, by binding their breasts, cutting their hair, and using charcoal on their faces to simulate a beard, lived in fear of being wounded and found out. Sarah Wakeman's secret was not discovered, but she did not survive the war. She died from dysentery in the Marine U.S.A. General Hospital in New Orleans on June 19, 1864.[9] She was buried in that city, in a grave bearing her masculine name.

▷ Packages From Home

The Union army was well equipped. Its soldiers were uniformed, fed, and supplied with arms and ammunition better than any previous force. Nonetheless, many soldiers depended on families and friends at home to provide familiar supplies, and most did not hesitate to be specific in their needs.

Thomas W. Smith, a member of the 6th Pennsylvania Cavalry, wrote a letter to his mother on January 26, 1862, with a list of things he wanted her to send. After

The 6th Pennsylvania Cavalry, to which Thomas Smith belonged, was the only regiment in the Union army to carry lances. Winslow Homer, working for *Harper's Weekly*, made this sketch of the regiment in Virginia in 1862. At **CivilWar@Smithsonian: Collections,** learn more about Homer's work as a "special artist" during the war.

EDITOR'S CHOICE

thanking her for keeping him informed of events at home and providing a gloomy weather report, Smith penned this "order" for supplies from home:

Another [of] the boys in our camp have been receiving boxes from home and now as I want some Tobacco I think I will get you to send me one. I want 3 1/2 lbs of Rough and Ready Tobacco. Tell Joe to get it at Fred Zimmerman's in Market St. above Eleventh and tell him that it is for me and to save him good moist tobacco. I want 25 sheats of Letter Paper and 25 Envelopes. Get them at Magees in Chesnit St above 3rd. Get them with Col Rush's Likeness on. If you have anything else in the way of Edibles to send you make

up a Box and send it by Addams Express. I will get it the day
after sent. So you need not be afraid of anything spoiling.[10]

Caring for the Soldiers

Over a million men moving from civilian jobs and homes
into military assignments wrote of concerns for their
health and their morals. Soldier's memoirs often com-
mented on how much drinking and gambling went on
during idle hours in camp between campaigns.

Lewis Richmond, assistant adjutant general for the
command of General Ambrose E. Burnside, stationed on
Roanoke Island, North Carolina, issued this general order
on February 15, 1862:

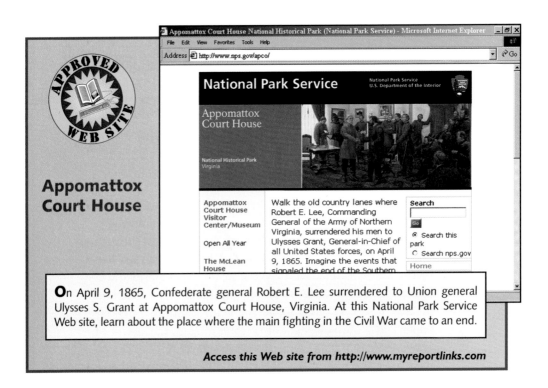

On April 9, 1865, Confederate general Robert E. Lee surrendered to Union general
Ulysses S. Grant at Appomattox Court House, Virginia. At this National Park Service
Web site, learn about the place where the main fighting in the Civil War came to an end.

Access this Web site from http://www.myreportlinks.com

In this department, whenever possible, Divine service will be held by the chaplains on Sunday, and on that day all work will cease excepting such as is absolutely necessary for the public service. The great trials and labors which have lately prevented the proper observance of this day being over, it is hoped that, in thankfulness for our preservation through the storms and the dangers we have passed and for the great victory granted us, all will join in the endeavor to keep it sacred.

In order to preserve the health of the command the brigade commanders will direct their troops to avoid as much as possible the swampy parts of the island, not to bathe in the sound before 9 o'clock in the morning or later than 3 in the afternoon, and not bathe or wash their clothes in swamp water, this practice engendering [producing] chills and fever.[11]

▷ Going Home

General Robert E. Lee surrendered the Army of Northern Virginia to General U. S. Grant at Appomattox Court House, Virginia, on April 9, 1865. Ten days later, General Joseph E. Johnston surrendered the Confederate Army of Tennessee at Bentonville, North Carolina, to General William T. Sherman. With the end of fighting, those soldiers who had managed to escape death, disease, or serious injury looked forward to returning to the lives they had led before the war.

Charles Gould's brother Richard wrote his sister Hannah on April 29 that "I am well and in good spirits, expecting to see home & all the folks in a month or

Selected Civil War Photographs

Access this Web site from http://www.myreportlinks.com

At this Web site from the Library of Congress, you can view its extensive collection of photographs from the Civil War.

EDITOR'S CHOICE

two." But Richard Gould also was saddened by the assassination of President Lincoln on April 14:

Well what do you think of the death of our noble President? I cannot find words to let you know what I think about it, so I will not try. This army was all alive with the good news till they heard of the death of Abe, and you cannot imagine the difference there was in our feelings.[12]

In the spring of 1865, the Union had been preserved through the leadership of Abraham Lincoln and the success of the Union army, but it had come at a great cost: About 360,000 Union soldiers had lost their lives in battle or from injuries or disease, and more than 275,000 were wounded but survived. And the United States faced the task of coming together as one nation, in a period known as Reconstruction, without the man whose leadership had helped preserve it.

Chapter 4 ▶

IN THE WORDS OF CONFEDERATE SOLDIERS

When secession came, men in the seceding states rushed to join state and then Confederate forces. So many wanted to enlist that the government asked some to go home and return later because they could not provide arms, uniforms, and other necessary supplies for all of them. After the fighting began, however, fewer men wanted to join the Confederate army, so then the Confederacy, like the Union, resorted to a military draft.

Some Confederates fought for the preservation of states' rights or other principles, but the majority enlisted

Robert E. Lee, once superintendent ▶ of the United States Military Academy at West Point, reluctantly resigned his commission with the U.S. Army to join the forces of the Confederacy.

because they believed that their homeland was being invaded and they needed to defend themselves. Few would have fought just to preserve slavery.

The Reverend J. William Jones was a twenty-four-year-old clergyman in Virginia when the Civil War began. He enlisted and later became a chaplain to the Army of Northern Virginia. He gave this dramatic description of the men who volunteered to fight for the Confederacy.

> The farmer leaves his plow in the furrow, the mechanic his job unfinished, the merchant his books unposted, the lawyer his brief unargued, the physician his patient unattended, the professor his chair unfilled, the student his classes, and the preacher his pulpit, and there rush to our northern frontier, not Hessian or Milesian mercenaries, not men bought up for so much "bounty money," but the wealth, the intelligence, the refinement and culture, the virtue and patriotism, the very flower of our Southern youth and manhood.[1]

Some Southerners joined the Confederate service only reluctantly. One was Colonel Robert E. Lee of Virginia, a decorated officer, Mexican-American War veteran, and past superintendent of the United States Military Academy at West Point. Lee, who initially opposed secession, was offered command of the Union army by Abraham Lincoln. But once his home state of Virginia seceded, Lee chose to fight on the side of his relatives and fellow Virginians who were at war with the Union. Lee wrote his sister, Mrs. William Marshall, about his difficult decision:

With all my devotion to the Union and the feeling of loyalty and duty of an American citizen, I have not been able to make up my mind to raise my hand against my relatives, my children, my home. I have therefore resigned my commission in the Army, and save in defence of my native state, with the sincere hope that my poor services may never be needed, I hope I may never be called on to draw my sword.[2]

▶ Leaving Home

Few Southerners traveled great distances before the Civil War, so those who left their homes to enter military service did so with a combination of anticipation and sadness. Community events to support the men in gray frequently involved flag presentations by local leaders and loved

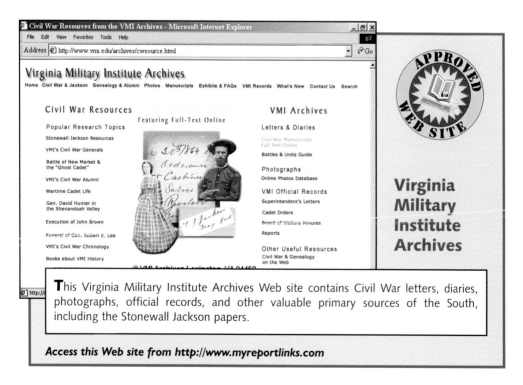

This Virginia Military Institute Archives Web site contains Civil War letters, diaries, photographs, official records, and other valuable primary sources of the South, including the Stonewall Jackson papers.

Access this Web site from http://www.myreportlinks.com

ones, but fears of never returning home were always in the thoughts of those leaving as well as those they left behind.

In the many letters he wrote home, Private Eli Pinson Landers of Gwinnett County, Georgia, echoed the excitement, boredom, and fear that were part of a soldier's life during the Civil War. He was nineteen when he enlisted in 1861 in Company H, Howell Cobb's 16th Regiment of Georgia Infantry Volunteers, known as the Flint Hill Grays. His enlistment was a hardship for his mother, a widow, who was left to work their farm. In his first letter to his brother, written on the day he departed from Georgia, he concluded, "But if I never see you again take care of yourself and I will try to do the same."[3] Four days later, from Virginia, Landers wrote to his mother:

I am now 7 hundred miles from you all. We ate breakfast in Augusta Monday morning. We got there about sun rise. The citizens of Augusta give us our breakfast and treated us well. There was a young lady give me a flag made of silk ribbon and told me to take it to Va [Virginia] but some grand raskal stold it. The people . . . give us the praise all the way. They hurahed for Georgia for she carrys the day here at Conier's Station. . . .

I have seed a heap [seen a lot] of sites since I left home more than I could write in a week and I went in a heap of dangers.[4]

Before 1861 ended, Landers had lost some of his enthusiasm for travel and for the war. On November 15, he wrote, "I have bin sick 6 weeks and have bin here 5 weeks today and no money and not well yet and I am

Like Eli Landers, William Askew was a private serving in a Georgia infantry division.

afraid that when I do get well I am afraid that being exposed as the poor solgers [soldiers] has to be, I am afraid that I will not get through the winter."[5]

In the next two years, Private Landers was involved in eight major battles, surviving Antietam, Chancellorsville, and Gettysburg among them. Twice wounded, he died in October 1863, but his death was from disease—typhoid fever—and not from injuries sustained in battle. In one of the last letters that Landers wrote to his mother, his fears were evident.

> My Dear Mother, if I never meet you again and should meet the dread fate of some of my friends I hope to meet you in a world of peace and pleasure. There is so many dangers staring me in the face I feel the need of a strong Protecter.[6]

The Life of a Confederate Soldier

Some soldiers liked the military life and wrote home about their adventures and experiences with enthusiasm.

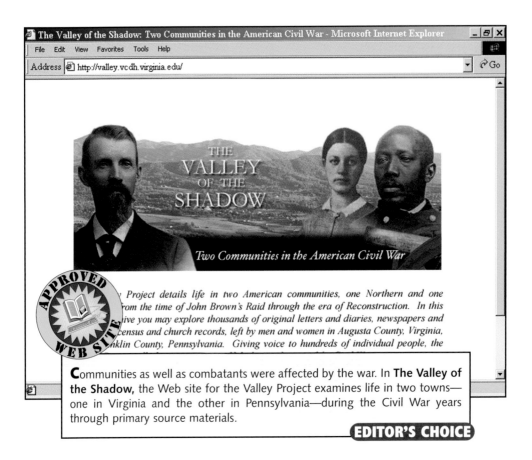

The Valley of the Shadow: Two Communities in the American Civil War - Microsoft Internet Explorer

File Edit View Favorites Tools Help

Address http://valley.vcdh.virginia.edu/

... Project details life in two American communities, one Northern and one *...from* the time of John Brown's Raid through the era of Reconstruction. In this *...ive* you may explore thousands of original letters and diaries, newspapers and *...census* and church records, left by men and women in Augusta County, Virginia, *...nklin* County, Pennsylvania. Giving voice to hundreds of individual people, the

Communities as well as combatants were affected by the war. In **The Valley of the Shadow,** the Web site for the Valley Project examines life in two towns—one in Virginia and the other in Pennsylvania—during the Civil War years through primary source materials.

EDITOR'S CHOICE

Marion Hill Fitzpatrick, another Georgian who served in the Army of Northern Virginia, wrote to his wife, Amanda, soon after entering the service and often thereafter. On May 11, 1862, Fitzpatrick wrote,

> We arrived safely here [Camp Anderson, Virginia] yesterday evening. I am well and getting on finely. I never enjoyed better health in my life. I have not even taken a cold. . . .

Later in the letter, Fitzpatrick informed his wife about his accommodations.

Jim Webb and I are staying in a tent with Jim Drue, at this time there [are] only four of us in the tent and we fare finely. I am well pleased so far. We get flour and bacon a plenty and have some of the best biscuits now out.[7]

Even later in the war when Fitzpatrick was hospitalized for an extended illness, he still bragged on the army's food:

We are doing better in the eating line now. We get fresh beef and mutton and pees [peas]. Not green garden pees but regular old fashioned red dried corn field pees. They go fine I tell you, and the beef or sheep is what I long have sought.

Fitzpatrick also was pleased with his wardrobe:

I have two shirts, two pr. Drawers, 1 pr. Pants, one blanket, one small oilcloth, and my overcoat with me. . . . I have three pr. Socks with me. . . .[8]

Learning of the Problems of Home

Letters from soldiers were filled with reports of health and camp life, and letters from those left behind informed absent servicemen of the trials of the home front.

Grant and Malinda Taylor of Alabama exchanged such information. Writing from Demopolis, Alabama, on April 13, 1862, Grant told Malinda that all was well:

We landed here Friday evening about 3 o'clock on the 11th and found 5 companies encamped on the fairground. We are very comfortably situated. We have good dry buildings to sleep in. We have a beautiful place to drill in but the regiment is not full and I am told that if [it] is not filled we will not stay here long but I do not know where. I should be very sorry to have to move as we are so well fixed.[9]

Malinda Taylor's letters were filled with practical reports.

I have had 25 bushels corn hald [hauled] and it cost me $405. I had to give dollar and quarter per bushel, $12 for halling, one dollar and half ferage [ferriage]. Mrs Goodsen hald for me and will hall another next week that will bee 50 bushels.

Malinda was most concerned, however, that her husband would return to her. She wrote: "Pray that God will bring you home safe. That is my greatist disire. Oh that I could know that you ever would get home in peace."[10]

◁ *General Robert E. Lee and his men survey the scene at Fredericksburg.*

Ordinary and Extraordinary Reports of Military Service

Serving in the Confederate army or any other army was characterized by a relatively few short times of intensive activity in campaigns and battles and longer periods of camp life that could be called boring.

Mark Smither, Company D, 5th Texas Infantry, wrote his brother about the hours that dragged on between moments of action:

> As I have nothing to do today I will seize the opportunity to write to you. We are leading, at the present time, rather a dull kind of life. It is eat, sleep, stand guard, (interspersed with a little drill when ever the weather will permit) from one days end to another. The weather is tolerably severe today and has been for some days past. The ground is covered with snow to the depth of about five inches but on the hillside it is nearly a foot deep. The boys are having a great deal of fun out doors snow balling and dunking each other in the snow.[11]

On the other hand, William R. Montgomery of Georgia described an intense moment in the Battle of Fredericksburg. He told of entrenching on the heights above Fredericksburg and watching General Ambrose E. Burnside's Union troops cross the Rappahannock River "to oppose our little handful of brave soldiers."[12]

Montgomery continued his account.

> Saturday [December 12, 1862] about 11 o'clock they began their advance & our brave & beloved Gen Cobb placed his

Private Philip Carper, of the 35th Battalion, Virginia Cavalry, appears in this ambrotype, an image produced by an inexpensive photographic process that allowed many soldiers to have their pictures taken for their loved ones.

Brigade behind a stone fence & pulled off his hat & waving it over his head exclaimed, "Get ready Boys here they come" & they did come *sure*.

We waited until they got within about 200 yards of us & rose to our feet & poured volley after volley into their ranks which told a most deadening effect. They soon began to waver & at last broke from the *rear,* but the shouts of our brave soldiers had scarcely died away when we saw coming another column more powerful & seemingly more determined than the first (if possible) but only a few rounds from our brave & well tried men was necessary to tell them that they had undertaken a work a little too hard. But before they had entirely left the field another column & another & still another came to their support. But our well aimed shots were more than they could stand so about night they were compelled to give up the field covered with their dead.[13]

Religion in the Confederate Army

Religious conversions were widespread in both the Confederate and Union camps during the years of the Civil War. The uncertain future faced by soldiers, particularly when lives were being lost in battle and to disease, helped spread a Christian revival. The Confederate army also included among its ranks many soldiers who were already devoutly religious and who believed the cause they were fighting for was "God's cause."

In 1864, the Reverend J. William Jones reported on the spiritual well-being of the Army of Northern Virginia.

> The religious condition of our army at present is both healthful and hopeful. Now that the weather has become unfavorable for frequent outdoor services, many of the regiments have neatly constructed log chapels, and many other chaplains, in lieu of this convenience, substitute the social prayer-meeting from hut to hut, Bible-classes, tract distribution, private conversation, etc., for the more public ministrations of the word. There is very great demand for good reading of all sorts, and the friends of the soldier can do nothing more acceptable to him than to send good books, papers, magazines, etc.[14]

Despite such mass religious worship, faith remained personal. In a letter written to her husband on December 28, 1862, Malinda Taylor showed how intense religious faith could be:

> Grant, you allways reque[s]t me to pray for you. Whenever, I com to the requst I dont read any ferther until I restle with God in your behalf. I b[e]lieve if prayers from the heart will save you, you will go through the struggle.[15]

Ending the War

Union advantages in manpower, equipment, and supplies began to prevail by mid-1863, and by early in 1865,

General U. S. Grant's army had General Robert E. Lee's command besieged at Petersburg, Virginia.

In the western theater, General William T. Sherman had captured the cities of Atlanta and Savannah, Georgia, and started northward through the Carolinas with little

This image of a Confederate soldier who lost his life in the trenches of Petersburg was taken in April 1865. The Civil War was the first war in which photography was widely used, and the images captured the brutality of the conflict.

resistance from Confederate General J. E. Johnston's army. Surrenders by Lee and Johnston in April sent soldiers still in the thin ranks homeward in defeat.

Confederate soldiers had to reach home on their own, whether a few or hundreds of miles distant, because their government had collapsed. Some made it, and some did not. And some soldiers' wives, such as Amanda Fitzpatrick, learned that they had become widows.

In June 1865, Amanda Fitzpatrick received a letter from a soldier named William Fields that informed her of her husband's death:

As you in all probability have not heard of the death of your husband and as I was a witness to his death I consider it my duty to write to you allthough I am a stranger to you. But your husband and myself have share[d] the same dangers under the same army for the past four years, allthough I did not get acquainted with him until he was wounded. Him and myself was wounded the same day the second of April and were brought to Richmond that night. . . . He died on the 6th of April, but I am happy to say he died happy and I certainly think that he is now better off. A few minutes before he breathed his last he sang Jesus can make a dying bed as soft as downy pillows are [lines from a hymn] & he said he would of liked to of seen you before he died. He said that the Lord's will be done and for you to meet him in heaven.[16]

Marion Hill Fitzpatrick was one of more than 260,000 Confederate soldiers who did not return home after the Civil War. Those who did, including more than 120,000 who returned wounded, faced serious challenges and great changes as the nation tried to reunite.

Chapter 5

THE WAR IN THE WORDS OF CIVILIANS

Before the invention of electronic communications such as telephone and e-mail, letters were the primary means of communicating with distant friends and family. People who wrote letters looked forward to receiving replies so that they could remain informed about family, personal, and public issues.

Chesnut, Mary Boykin Miller. "A Diary From Dixie" - Microsoft Internet Explorer

File   Edit   View   Favorites   Tools   Help

Address http://docsouth.unc.edu/chesnut/frontis.html

A portrait of Mary Chesnut, whose diary offers a vivid account of one Southern woman's life during the war. **Documenting the American South** contains digital images and primary source documents of Southern life during the conflict.

EDITOR'S CHOICE

Many wrote daily in diaries and journals for their own record of past events, never expecting others to gain access to such intimate thoughts. So during the Civil War, it was natural for Union and Confederate civilians to record their hopes, fears, and reactions to the success or failure of their governments.

The Voice of a Southern Woman

Colonel James Chesnut served as a negotiator for Confederate general P. G. T. Beauregard with Major Robert Anderson, commander of Fort Sumter. South Carolina and the Confederate governments believed that the federal government should release its property in the South, such as this fort, to them.

For days, Anderson said that he would surrender but only after he had used up his supplies. Growing weary of delays, on April 11, 1861, Beauregard told Chesnut to start firing on the fort if Anderson would not set the date for the surrender. From Charleston, Chesnut's wife, Mary Boykin Chesnut, recorded her reaction to the events of April 12:

I do not pretend to go to sleep. How can I? If Anderson does not accept terms—at four [a.m.]—the orders are—he shall be fired upon.

I count four—St. Michael chimes. I begin to hope. At half-past four, the heavy booming of a cannon.

I sprang out of bed. And on my knees—prostrate—I prayed as I never prayed before. . . .

I knew my husband was rowing about in a boat somewhere in that dark bay. And that the shells were roofing it over—bursting toward the fort. . . .

The women were wild, there on the housetop. Prayers from the women and imprecations from the men, and then a shell would light up the scene.[1]

The next day, Mary Chesnut had this to say about the reaction of the slaves in her household to the firing on Fort Sumter:

Not by one word or look can we detect any change in the demeanor of these negro servants. Laurence sits at our door, as sleepy and as respectful and as profoundly indifferent. So are they all. They carry it too far. You could not tell that they hear even the awful row that is going on in the bay, though it is dinning in their ears night and day. And people talk before them as if they were chairs and tables. And they make no sign. Are they stolidly stupid or wiser than we are, silent and strong, biding their time?[2]

The Voice of a Northern Man

In his diary entry for April 15, 1861, New York lawyer George Templeton Strong put down his reaction to the news that Confederates had fired on Fort Sumter and initiated the Civil War:

Events multiply. The President is out with a proclamation calling for 75,000 volunteers and an extra session of Congress July 4. It is said 200,000 more will be called within a few days. Every man of them will be wanted before this game is lost or won. . . . Everybody's patriotism is rampant and demonstrative now.[3]

"A tall, lank, lean man . . . [with a] strange quaint face and head. . . . " was how British newspaper correspondent William Howard Russell described Abraham Lincoln.

The next day, Strong wrote, "GOD SAVE THE UNION, AND CONFOUND ITS ENEMIES. AMEN."[4]

A View From Afar

William Howard Russell, a British correspondent for the *Times* of London, crossed the Atlantic Ocean in 1861 to report on America's Civil War for English readers.

In addition to his reports for his paper, Russell kept a diary during his travels, which included extended visits in both Union and Confederate states. Among his interesting observations are these personal descriptions of United States president Abraham Lincoln and Confederate president Jefferson Davis.

Of Lincoln, whom Russell visited in the White House, he said,

Soon afterward there entered, with a shambling, loose, irregular, almost unsteady gait, a tall, lank, lean man, considerably over six feet in height, with stooping shoulders, long pendulous arms, terminating in hands of extraordinary dimensions, which, however, were far exceeded in proportion by his feet. He was dressed in an ill-fitting, wrinkled suit of black, which put one in mind of an undertaker's uniform at a funeral; round his neck a rope of black silk was knotted in a large bulb, with flying ends projecting beyond the collar of his coat; his turned-down shirt collar disclosed a sinewy muscular yellow neck, and above that, nestling in a great black mass of hair, bristling and compact like a riff of mourning pins, rose the strange quaint face and head, covered with its thatch of wild republican hair, of President Lincoln.[5]

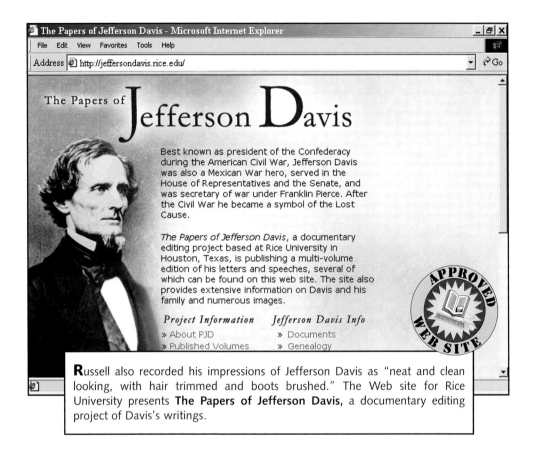

The Papers of Jefferson Davis - Microsoft Internet Explorer

File   Edit   View   Favorites   Tools   Help

Address http://jeffersondavis.rice.edu/

The Papers of Jefferson Davis

Best known as president of the Confederacy during the American Civil War, Jefferson Davis was also a Mexican War hero, served in the House of Representatives and the Senate, and was secretary of war under Franklin Pierce. After the Civil War he became a symbol of the Lost Cause.

The Papers of Jefferson Davis, a documentary editing project based at Rice University in Houston, Texas, is publishing a multi-volume edition of his letters and speeches, several of which can be found on this web site. The site also provides extensive information on Davis and his family and numerous images.

Project Information   *Jefferson Davis Info*

» About PJD   » Documents
» Published Volumes   » Genealogy

Russell also recorded his impressions of Jefferson Davis as "neat and clean looking, with hair trimmed and boots brushed." The Web site for Rice University presents **The Papers of Jefferson Davis,** a documentary editing project of Davis's writings.

Russell visited President Jefferson Davis in Richmond and recorded these impressions:

I had an opportunity of observing the President very closely: he did not impress me as favorably as I had expected, though he is certainly a very different looking man from Mr. Lincoln. He is like a gentleman—has a slight, light figure, little exceeding middle height, and holds himself erect and straight. He was dressed in a rustic suit of slate-coloured stuff, with a black silk handkerchief round his neck; his manner is plain, and rather reserved and drastic; his head is well-formed, with a fine full forehead, square and high, covered with innumerable fine lines and wrinkles, features regular, though the cheek-bones are too high, and the jaws too hollow to be handsome; the lips are thin, flexible, and curved, the chin square, well defined; the nose very regular, with wide nostrils; and the eyes deep set, large and full— one seems nearly blind, and is partly covered with a film, owing to excruciating attacks of neuralgia and tic. Wonderful to relate, he does not chew [tobacco], and is neat and clean-looking, with hair trimmed and boots brushed. The expression . . . is anxious, he has a very haggard, care-worn, and pain-drawn look, though no trace of anything but the utmost confidence and greatest decision could be detected in his conversation.[6]

Dissent in the North

Not everyone who lived in the Northern states supported the Lincoln administration's efforts to force the seceded

A LITTLE GAME OF BAGATELLE, BETWEEN OLD ABE THE RAIL SPLITTER & LITTLE MAC THE GUNBOAT GENERAL.

▲ This political cartoon from 1864 depicts the presidential election of that year as a game of bagatelle (a game like pool) between candidates Abraham Lincoln and George McClellan. Clement Vallandigham, leader of the Copperheads, pro-Confederate Northerners, is pictured seated at right.

states to return to the Union. One who did not was Clement L. Vallandigham, a Democratic political leader in Ohio. Writing in 1863, Vallandigham summed up the Lincoln administration's lack of progress in the Civil War:

> And now, sir, I recur [return in thought] to the state of the Union to-day. What is it? Sir, twenty months have elapsed, but the rebellion is not crushed out; its military power has not been broken; the insurgents have not dispersed. The Union is not restored; nor the Constitution maintained; nor the laws enforced. Twenty, sixty, ninety, three hundred, six hundred days have passed; a thousand millions have been expended; and three hundred thousand lives lost or bodies mangled; and to-day the Confederate flag is still near the Potomac and the Ohio, and the Confederate Government stronger, many times, than at the beginning. Not a state has been restored, nor any part of any State has voluntarily returned to the Union.[7]

Unhappiness in the Confederacy

John B. Jones, a clerk in the Confederate Department of War, was also an editor and novelist. He kept a diary rich with information about happenings in the Confederate capital. His diary entry for May 23, 1862, documents the impact of inflation on the Southern economy:

> Oh, the extortioners! Meats of all kinds are selling at fifty cents per pound; butter, seventy-five cents; coffee, a dollar and half; tea, ten dollars; boots, thirty dollars per pair; shoes, eighteen dollars; ladies' shoes, fifteen dollars; shirts, six dollars each. Houses that rented for five hundred dollars last year are a thousand dollars now. Boarding, from thirty

to forty dollars per month. General [John Henry] Winder [provost marshal of Richmond], has issued an order fixing the maximum prices of certain articles of marketing, which has only the effect of keeping a great many things out of market.[8]

▶ Victory and Tragedy in the North

Learning that Union troops had finally captured the Confederate capital of Richmond, Maria Daly, a prominent New Yorker, recorded her reaction to the good news in her diary entry for April 5, 1865:

Richmond is ours! Lee is retreating! . . . The streets are brilliant with flags. On Saturday when the news came, there was an impromptu meeting in Wall Street. All business adjourned, a few speeches, and then the multitude sang the Doxology and the 100th Psalm in Wall Street, the seat of the money-changers; it was a good augury [sign]. When I got the extra [special newspaper edition] containing the great news, the tears rushed to my eyes, my heart to my throat. I could not speak. . . . May God's blessing come with it [peace] and make us less a money-loving, selfish, and self-sufficient people, purified by this great trial. . . .[9]

But happiness gave way to sorrow following John Wilkes Booth's assassination of President Abraham Lincoln at Ford's Theatre in Washington, D.C., on April 14, 1865. The following day, the African-American abolitionist Frederick Douglass, who had often criticized the president early in the war for not moving fast enough

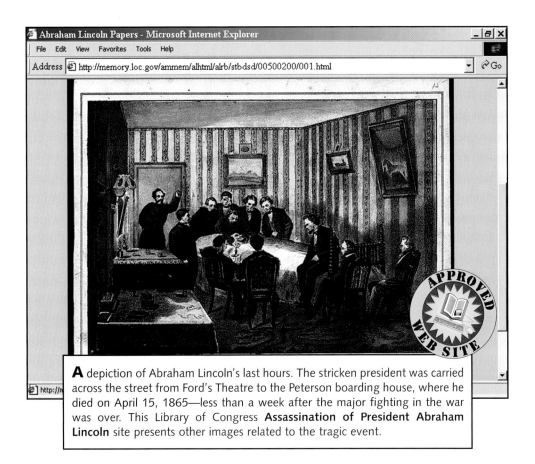

Abraham Lincoln Papers - Microsoft Internet Explorer

File   Edit   View   Favorites   Tools   Help

Address http://memory.loc.gov/ammem/alhtml/alrb/stbdsd/00500200/001.html   Go

http://

A depiction of Abraham Lincoln's last hours. The stricken president was carried across the street from Ford's Theatre to the Peterson boarding house, where he died on April 15, 1865—less than a week after the major fighting in the war was over. This Library of Congress **Assassination of President Abraham Lincoln** site presents other images related to the tragic event.

toward emancipation, mourned and praised the president in an address he gave in Rochester, New York.

A dreadful disaster has befallen the nation. It is a day for silence and meditation; for grief and tears. Yet I feel that though Abraham Lincoln dies, the Republic lives; though that great and good man, one of the noblest men [to] trod God's earth, is struck down by the hand of the assassin, yet I know that the nation is saved and liberty established forever.[10]

Collapse of the Confederacy

President Jefferson Davis and his cabinet escaped from Richmond just before Union forces occupied the Confederate capital. Within a few days, General Robert E. Lee surrendered the Army of Northern Virginia to Union forces commanded by General Ulysses S. Grant at Appomattox Court House, Virginia. Other Confederate military units surrendered within a month, ending the effort to establish an independent government in the South.

Mary Boykin Chesnut, whose diary is among the best historical accounts of the Confederate experience, wrote of the anxiety of Southerners in the unsettled circumstances following the war's end. Mrs. Chesnut described the change in attitude of a clergyman:

Yesterday a fiery parson who has always preached blood and thunder from his pulpit—drum ecclesiastic beat with fist instead of a stick—was as peaceful as a dove. He advised his congregation "to cultivate a submissive spirit and to betake themselves quietly to agricultural pursuits."

And does he think, after four years fighting as men never fought before, after killing more of their men than we ever had in the field— Burton Harrison said the Yankee

Areas of the South lay in ruins by the war's end.

dead were over three hundred thousand—does he think they will let us quietly slide back into the old grooves as we were before?[11]

Mrs. Chesnut judged correctly that Southerners would have to endure a difficult period of readjustment to become citizens of the United States again. Her diary entry for May 16, 1865—approximately one month after the collapse of the Confederacy—shows the bewilderment of defeated Southerners:

We are scattered—stunned—the remnant of heart left alive with us, filled with brotherly hate. . . .

We sit and wait until the drunken tailor who rules the U.S.A. [President Andrew Johnson, who succeeded to the presidency following the death of President Lincoln] issues a proclamation and defines our anomalous [peculiar] position.

Such a hue and cry—whose fault? Everybody blamed by somebody else. Only the dead heroes left stiff and stark on the battlefield escape.

"Blame every man who stayed at home and did not fight. I will not stop to hear excuses. Not one word against those who stood out until the bitter end and stacked muskets at Appomattox."[12]

Two days later, Mrs. Chesnut wrote, "A feeling of sadness hovers over me now, day and night, that no words of mine can express."[13] Yet her words and the words of others who lived through the war give us the truest possible sense of what life was really like during America's Civil War.

Chapter 6

THE WAR IN SONG

The warm glow of a campfire drew the men closer. The day's march had been hard, and before supper there was plenty of dust to shake off clothes and sometimes it seemed from the soul.

Shoulders ached from the weight of packs, feet hurt from picking them up and laying them down again a million times or more, and a gnawing feeling in the midsection reminded the soldiers of too much work and too little sleep and food.

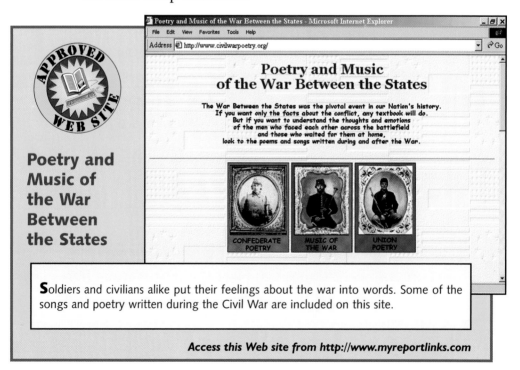

Poetry and Music of the War Between the States - Microsoft Internet Explorer

File   Edit   View   Favorites   Tools   Help

Address http://www.civilwarpoetry.org/   Go

Poetry and Music of the War Between the States

The War Between the States was the pivotal event in our Nation's history.
If you want only the facts about the conflict, any textbook will do.
But if you want to understand the thoughts and emotions
of the men who faced each other across the battlefield
and those who waited for them at home,
look to the poems and songs written during and after the War.

CONFEDERATE POETRY   MUSIC OF THE WAR   UNION POETRY

Poetry and Music of the War Between the States

Soldiers and civilians alike put their feelings about the war into words. Some of the songs and poetry written during the Civil War are included on this site.

Access this Web site from http://www.myreportlinks.com

But the fire was warm, and friends were near. Someone began to hum, and one tapped rhythm on his boot. Presently a banjo came out and the clear precision of its staccato harmony gave a bouncy turn to a familiar song; soon everyone was singing.

They sang for a while, until each was captured by his thoughts. The music had helped; it uplifted, sustained, cheered, reindoctrinated, saddened. It was as much of their soldiering as the sergeant's curse and the officer's starch.

This could describe either a Union or Confederate camp because both sides in the Civil War enjoyed and used music to boost morale, to convince themselves of their righteousness, or just as a way to get through the war.

Music of the Civil War

More than ten thousand songs were written by Union and Confederate musicians and poets during the four years of America's Civil War. Most were published in the North, the prewar center of all kinds of publishing in the United States. Publishing houses were founded in the Confederacy, but they had to cope with such problems as shortages of ink and paper.[1]

Soldiers in both armies carried "songsters," or small volumes containing only the lyrics of songs, in their knapsacks. Only the Bible exceeded these "songsters" in popularity with the men.

Songs Dear to Soldiers in Gray

The lyrics to "The Bonnie Blue Flag," the first song to capture the fancy of Confederates, were written by the

English stage performer Harry Macarthy and introduced into his act in Jackson, Mississippi. Like many Civil War songs, Macarthy's songs included lyrics that could be sung to music written previously, in this case a tune known as "The Irish Jaunting Car."

There are several explanations why Macarthy wrote "The Bonnie Blue Flag." The most popular explanation is that Macarthy was moved after witnessing C. R. Dickson, the postmaster of Jackson, Mississippi, carrying a blue flag with a single white star at Mississippi's secession convention.

South Carolina adopted a similar flag at its secession convention, and some believe that this inspired Macarthy's creativity. Others say that he simply wrote it to take advantage of the martial spirit swelling in the South. "The Bonnie Blue Flag" has many verses, but this is the most famous:

We are a band of brothers, and native to the soil,

Fighting for the property we gained by honest toil;

And when our rights were threatened, the cry rose near and far:

"Hurrah for the Bonnie Blue Flag that bears a single star!"

Hurrah! Hurrah! For Southern rights, hurrah!

Hurrah for the Bonnie Blue Flag that bears a single star.[2]

"Maryland, My Maryland"

The poem "Maryland, My Maryland," written by James R. Randall, captured interest throughout the Confederacy. Randall, a native of Baltimore, was teaching at Poydras

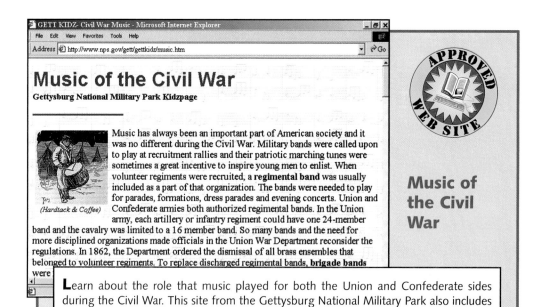

Music of the Civil War

Gettysburg National Military Park Kidzpage

Music has always been an important part of American society and it was no different during the Civil War. Military bands were called upon to play at recruitment rallies and their patriotic marching tunes were sometimes a great incentive to inspire young men to enlist. When volunteer regiments were recruited, a **regimental band** was usually included as a part of that organization. The bands were needed to play for parades, formations, dress parades and evening concerts. Union and Confederate armies both authorized regimental bands. In the Union army, each artillery or infantry regiment could have one 24-member band and the cavalry was limited to a 16 member band. So many bands and the need for more disciplined organizations made officials in the Union War Department reconsider the regulations. In 1862, the Department ordered the dismissal of all brass ensembles that belonged to volunteer regiments. To replace discharged regimental bands, **brigade bands** were

(Hardtack & Coffee)

Music of the Civil War

Learn about the role that music played for both the Union and Confederate sides during the Civil War. This site from the Gettysburg National Military Park also includes sound files of some of the more popular songs and provides written lyrics for each.

Access this Web site from http://www.myreportlinks.com

College, Pointe Coupée, Louisiana, when Union troops occupied Baltimore to prevent Maryland from seceding.

Randall wrote his poem in honor of the citizens of his hometown who defied federal occupiers, hoping it would inspire Marylanders to secede and join the Confederacy. Jennie Cary adapted Randall's poem to the music of "O Tannenbaum":

> *The despot's heel is on thy shore,*
>
> *Maryland, my Maryland!*
>
> *His torch is at thy temple door,*
>
> *Maryland, my Maryland!*
>
> *Avenge the patriotic gore,*
>
> *That flecked the streets of Baltimore,*

And be the battle queen of yore,

Maryland, my Maryland![3]

The popularity of Randall's song inspired numerous imitations, including this Union response written by Sep Winner of Philadelphia:

The Rebel horde is on thy shore,

Maryland, my Maryland!

Arise and drive him from thy door,

Maryland, my Maryland![4]

"The Bonnie Blue Flag" and "Maryland, My Maryland" became immensely popular (and "Maryland, My Maryland" became Maryland's state song in 1939), but no song captured the hearts of Southerners quite like Daniel Decatur Emmett's "Dixie," or "In Dixie's Land."

Emmett, who grew up in the rough frontier land that was Ohio early in the 1800s, wrote the song in 1859 for Bryant's Minstrels, a singing group he was performing with in New York. (American minstrel shows were made up of white performers in blackface—wearing makeup to appear black—who impersonated black singers and comedians.)

▶ In the Land of Dixie

"Dixie" was introduced in the South in New Orleans and was played at the inauguration of Jefferson Davis. It was also the song that Abraham Lincoln requested to be played for him on the night that Union forces occupied

Richmond. At the outset of the war, it was popular in both Union and Confederate camps, but it soon became firmly identified with the South, much to Emmett's displeasure (since he supported the Union). The following lyrics were the first published version of the song, written in the dialect that minstrels used in their attempts to sound like African Americans.

I wish I was in de land ob cotton,

Old times dar am not forgotten, Look away!

Look away! Look away! Dixie Land.

In Dixie land whar I was born in,

Early on one frosty mornin, Look away!

Look away! Look away! Dixie Land.

Chorus:
Den I wish I was in Dixie, Hooray! Hooray!

In Dixie Land I'll take my stand,

To lib an die in Dixie.

Away, Away, Away down south in Dixie.

Away, Away, Away down south in Dixie.[5]

▶ Songs Dear to Soldiers in Blue

The citizens and soldiers from Northern states had their own rousing songs to rally support for the war effort and boost soldiers' morale. George F. Root, a native of Massachusetts and a respected musician, wrote one of the most beloved war songs of all time:

"The Battle Cry of Freedom." It was introduced in Chicago at a war rally on July 24, 1862, by the Lumbard Brothers, a vocal group. Root's song became immensely popular throughout the North, especially with Union soldiers, and was as well known by its first line—"Oh, we'll rally 'round the flag, boys"—as by its actual title. The first verse and refrain follow.

Yes we'll rally round the flag, boys, we'll rally once again,

Shouting the battle-cry of freedom,

And we bear the glorious stars for the Union and the right,

Shouting the battle-cry of freedom.

Refrain:
The Union forever, Hurrah! boys, Hurrah!

Down with the traitor, up with the star,

For we're marching to the field, boys, going to the fight,

Shouting the battle-cry of freedom![6]

The song had an important impact on Southern troops as well. A Confederate major wrote:

I shall never forget the first time that I heard "Rally 'Round the Flag." Twas a nasty night during the "Seven Days Fight," and . . . it was raining. I was on picket when, just before taps, some fellow on the other side struck up that song and others joined in the chorus until it seemed to me the whole Yankee Army was singing. . . . I am not naturally superstitious, but I tell you that song sounded to me like the "knell of doom," and my heart went down into my boots; and

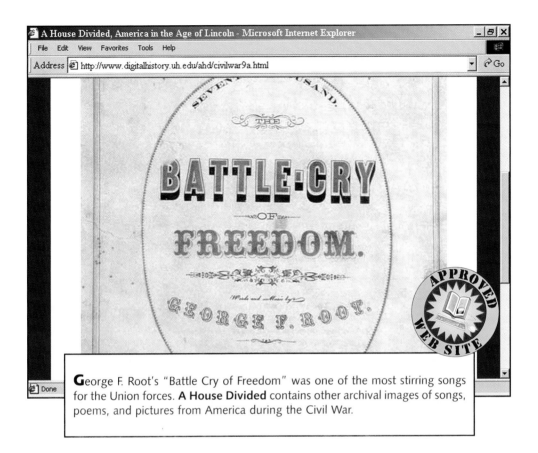

George F. Root's "Battle Cry of Freedom" was one of the most stirring songs for the Union forces. **A House Divided** contains other archival images of songs, poems, and pictures from America during the Civil War.

though I've tried to do my duty, it has been an uphill fight with me ever since that night.[7]

"Marching Through Georgia," written by Henry Clay Work, celebrated one of the Union's most successful campaigns. After capturing Atlanta in September 1864, General William T. Sherman abandoned his supply base there and marched his army across Georgia to Savannah. Sherman provided for his army with supplies seized from civilians along the way, and his "bummers" destroyed property they did not confiscate.

Here are two verses from Work's "Marching Through Georgia":

Bring the good old bugle, boys, we'll sing another song,

Sing it with the spirit that will start the world along,

Sing it as we used to sing it, fifty thousand strong,

While we were marching through Georgia.

Chorus:
Hurrah! Hurrah! We bring the jubilee!

Hurrah! Hurrah! The flag that makes you free!

So we sang the chorus from Atlanta to the sea,

While we were marching through Georgia!

So we made a thoroughfare for Freedom and her train,

Sixty miles in latitude, three hundred to the main;

Treason fled before us, for resistance was in vain,

While we were marching through Georgia.[8]

Julia Ward Howe's poem "The Battle Hymn of the Republic" was written in November 1861 and set to the music of a Methodist hymn. The hymn's music had already been used two years earlier as the tune for the song "John Brown's Body."

Howe wrote the poem while visiting army camps with her husband, Dr. Samuel Gridley Howe, a member of the U.S. Sanitary Commission, a relief organization that was set up by private citizens to help soldiers. She did so after

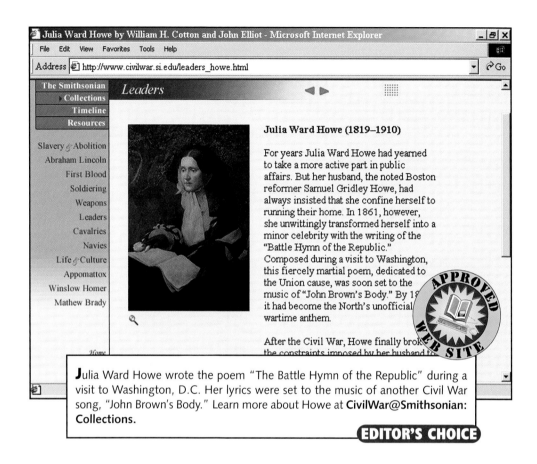

Julia Ward Howe by William H. Cotton and John Elliot - Microsoft Internet Explorer

File   Edit   View   Favorites   Tools   Help

Address http://www.civilwar.si.edu/leaders_howe.html

The Smithsonian
Collections
Timeline
Resources

Slavery & Abolition
Abraham Lincoln
First Blood
Soldiering
Weapons
Leaders
Cavalries
Navies
Life & Culture
Appomattox
Winslow Homer
Mathew Brady

Leaders

Julia Ward Howe (1819–1910)

For years Julia Ward Howe had yearned to take a more active part in public affairs. But her husband, the noted Boston reformer Samuel Gridley Howe, had always insisted that she confine herself to running their home. In 1861, however, she unwittingly transformed herself into a minor celebrity with the writing of the "Battle Hymn of the Republic." Composed during a visit to Washington, this fiercely martial poem, dedicated to the Union cause, was soon set to the music of "John Brown's Body." By 18__ it had become the North's unofficial wartime anthem.

After the Civil War, Howe finally bro__ the constraints imposed by her husband t__

Home

APPROVED WEB SITE

Julia Ward Howe wrote the poem "The Battle Hymn of the Republic" during a visit to Washington, D.C. Her lyrics were set to the music of another Civil War song, "John Brown's Body." Learn more about Howe at **CivilWar@Smithsonian: Collections.**

EDITOR'S CHOICE

the Reverend James Freeman Clarke suggested she write more appropriate words to "John Brown's Body."

Mrs. Howe reported,

In spite of the excitement of the day I went to bed and slept as usual, but awoke next morning in the gray of the early dawn, and to my astonishment found that the wished-for lines were arranging themselves in my brain. I lay quite still until the last verse had completed itself in my thoughts, then hastily arose, saying to myself, "I shall lose this if I don't write it down immediately." I searched for an old sheet of paper and an old stump of a pen . . . and began to scrawl the lines almost without looking. . . . Having completed this, I lay down again and fell asleep, but not without feeling that something of importance had happened to me.[9]

The first verse and chorus of "The Battle Hymn of the Republic" follow.

Mine eyes have seen the glory of the coming of the Lord;

He is trampling out the vintage where the grapes of wrath are stored,

He hath loosed the fateful lightning of His terrible swift sword,

His truth is marching on.

Chorus:
Glory, Glory, Hallelujah

Glory, Glory, Hallelujah,

Glory, Glory, Hallelujah,

His truth is marching on.[10]

▶ Special Songs of the Civil War

Not every song that became popular during the Civil War was inspiring or even serious. A happy song that eased the boredom of camp life and helped to relieve stress for many Southern soldiers was "Goober Peas," a song that takes its name from a Southern term for *peanut.* The lyrics for this parody, according to the sheet music, were written by "A. Pindar," a dialect word for peanut, and the music was composed by "P. Nutt, Esq." Here are sample verses:

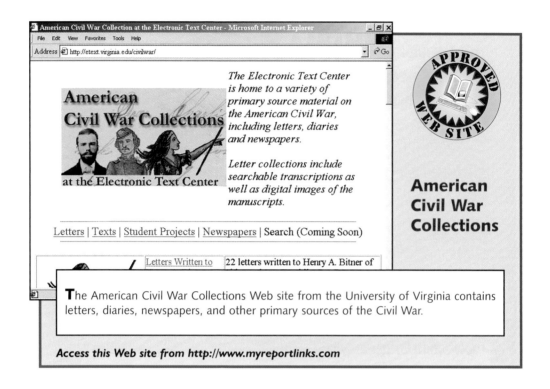

The American Civil War Collections Web site from the University of Virginia contains letters, diaries, newspapers, and other primary sources of the Civil War.

Access this Web site from http://www.myreportlinks.com

Sitting by the roadside, on a summer's day,

Chatting with my messmates, passing time away,

Lying in the shadow, underneath the trees,

Goodness how delicious, eating goober peas.

Chorus:
Peas! Peas! Peas! Peas! Eating goober peas!

Goodness how delicious, Eating goober peas!

Just before the battle, the Gen'ral hears a row,

He says, "The Yanks are coming, I hear their rifles now."

He turns around in wonder, and what do you think he sees?

The Georgia Militia—eating goober peas![11]

One of the saddest songs to come out of the Civil War was "Just Before the Battle, Mother," written by George F. Root. Written in support of the Union, it was also popular among Confederate soldiers. Its words, unfortunately, rang true for both sides. The song is presented as a letter written by a soldier to his mother on the eve of a battle he does not expect to survive:

> *Just before the battle, Mother,*
> *I am thinking most of you.*
> *While upon the field we're watching,*
> *With the enemy in view.*
> *Comrades brave are 'round me lying,*
> *Filled with thoughts of home and God,*
> *For well they know that on the morrow,*
> *Some will sleep beneath the sod.*
>
> Chorus:
> *Farewell, Mother, you may never,*
> *Press me to your breast again;*
> *But, Oh, you'll not forget me, Mother,*
> *If I'm numbered with the slain.*[12]

▲ *The band of the 107th U.S. Colored Infantry, Fort Corcoran.*

PRESS COVERAGE AND OFFICIAL ACCOUNTS OF THE WAR

Journalism in the Civil War era differed from modern journalism in many ways. For one thing, even small towns supported one or more newspapers, and larger cities hosted as many as a dozen. These papers often took bold stands on the political issues of the day, depending on the views of the editor. Often, the editor's opinions appeared on the front page of the newspaper, rather than in a designated section located inside.[1]

William Lloyd Garrison's abolitionist newspaper the *Liberator,* published in Boston, existed exclusively to oppose slavery. Horace Greeley's *New York Tribune* came as close as the United States has ever come to having a national newspaper, and in the South, Robert Barwell Rhett's *Charleston Mercury* presented the South's views on slavery, states' rights, and secession for its entire region.

Reporters visited military encampments freely, and the swiftness of the telegraph allowed their reports a sense of immediacy for readers. Sometimes those reports contained information that proved useful to their opponents. Confederate general Robert E. Lee read every Northern newspaper he could obtain and often made his own decisions about the Union army based on information obtained from them.[2]

Artists were hired by newspapers and magazines to sketch scenes of battle. This sketch shows Union troops crossing Antietam Creek. It appeared in the October 11, 1862, edition of *Frank Leslie's Illustrated Newspaper,* a weekly that combined news and illustrations. View more images at the **Antietam National Battlefield Image Gallery,** a National Park Service Web page.

Front pages of the *Charleston Mercury* and the *New York Times,* a major daily paper, presented differing viewpoints of these pivotal events in the Civil War.

▶ Firing on Fort Sumter

The first armed clash of the war, at Fort Sumter, in Charleston Harbor, received the following coverage in the *Charleston Mercury* on April 15, 1861:

We closed the report of the grand military diorama in progress on our Bay amid the clouds and gloom and threatening perils of Friday night. The firing, abated in the early evening, as though for the concentration of its special energies, commenced again at ten o'clock, and amid gusts of rain, and clouds that swept the heavens, the red hot shot and lighted shells, again streamed from the girt of batteries around and concentrated in fearful import over Fort Sumter. . . .[3]

The paper's reaction to the surrender of the fort appeared later, on the same page:

The rest is briefly told. Col. [Louis T.] Wigfall returned and notified the Captains of the several companies to inform their respective commands that the fort was unconditionally surrendered.

Alfred R. Waud was a sketch artist working for *Harper's Weekly*. Here he is photographed near Devil's Den, shortly after the Battle of Gettysburg. At **The Civil War Home Page,** learn more about the artists whose works brought the war home to readers.

The scene that followed was altogether indescribable. The troops upon the hills cheered and cheered again. A horseman galloped at full speed along the beach, waving his cap to troops near the Lighthouse. These soon caught up the cry, and the whole shore rang with the glad shouts of thousands.[4]

On the same day, the *New York Times* reported the loss of Fort Sumter this way:

It is by no means impossible, after all, that what seemed at first to be a national calamity, and which rendered yesterday a memorably dark day in the experience of every patriot, was after all a substantial and crowning advantage, anticipated and provided for in the plans of the Administration. Its policy has been uniform and consistent—to protect the property of the Government, and enforce its laws. It will yield nothing belonging to it unless dispossessed by superior force, but it will not weaken the reputation of its military arm, by a reckless waste of men or means in the maintenance or attempted recapture of any comparatively valueless position.[5]

▶ The Battle of Chancellorsville

The Army of the Potomac, led by General Joseph Hooker, and General Robert E. Lee's Army of Northern Virginia clashed in Virginia at Chancellorsville, near Fredericksburg, on May 2, 1863. This was Lee's last significant victory of the war, but it came with a terrible cost—the wounding and subsequent death of General T. J. "Stonewall" Jackson, Lee's most competent corps commander, on May 10.

The death of Thomas "Stonewall" Jackson was a great loss to the Confederacy. Southern newspapers described Lee's ablest general in legendary terms.

The *Charleston Mercury* pointed out on Wednesday, May 13, that Lee was the central figure of Southern arms,

But JACKSON was the motive power that executed, with the rapidity of lightning, all that LEE could plan. LEE has been the exponent of Southern power of command; JACKSON, the expression of its faith in God and in itself, its terrible energy, its enthusiasm and daring, its unconquerable will, its contempt of danger and fatigue, its capacity to smite [strike down], as with bolts of thunder, the cowardly and cruel foe that would trample under foot its liberty and its religion.[6]

Although the loss at Chancellorsville caused President Abraham Lincoln to replace General Joseph Hooker with General George Gordon Meade, the *New York Times* on Friday, May 8, reported the battle this way:

It is ascertained [found out] from the front that the Army of the Potomac has arrived, with all its material, at their old camps at Falmouth.

The demonstration of Gen. Hooker has proved no disaster, but simply a failure, owing to the impracticability of the position which the army had gained with so much skill and energy. Less than three-eighths of the whole force was engaged as could be engaged, the ground being covered with forest, and being without any practicable roads.

Our entire loss in killed, wounded and missing does not exceed 10,000. The enemy's loss must have been double of this—honorably to the army, but lamentably for the country, the greatest proportion of them in killed and wounded.[7]

The Battle of Atlanta

General William T. Sherman's victory over Southern forces in Atlanta in September 1864 ended a long campaign that had begun in southeastern Tennessee. The loss of Atlanta led to the destruction of the Army of Tennessee, the Confederacy's principal force in the western theater.

The campaign to capture Atlanta, and especially General Sherman's March to the Sea, or to Savannah, on Georgia's Atlantic coast, involved many civilians as well.

Before attacking Atlanta, Sherman proposed the removal of as many civilians as possible from harm's way. Southern commander General John Bell Hood objected, and the *New York Times* published Sherman's reply. In part, Sherman said,

> I have the honor to acknowledge the receipt of your letter . . . consenting to the arrangements I had proposed to facilitate the removal south of the people of Atlanta who prefer to go in that direction. I enclose you a copy of my orders, which will, I am satisfied accomplish my purpose perfectly. You style the measures proposed "unprecedented," and appeal to the dark history of war for a parallel as an act of "studied and ungenerous cruelty." It is not unprecedented, for General [Joseph E.] Johnston [Hood's predecessor] himself very wisely and properly removed the families all the way from

William Tecumseh Sherman was often cast as the destroyer of the South, but in truth the policy of total war that he followed was set by Ulysses S. Grant.

Dalton down, and I see no reason why Atlanta should be excepted [*sic*]. Nor is it necessary to appeal to the dark history of war when recent and modern examples are so handy. You, yourself, burned dwelling-houses . . . that you have rendered uninhabitable because they stood in the way of your forts and men.

. . . If we must be enemies, let us be men, and fight it out as we propose to-day, and not deal in such hypocritical appeals to God and humanity. God will judge us in due time, and he will pronounce whether it be more humane to fight with a town full of women and the families of a "brave people" at our back, or to remove them in time to places of safety among their own friends and people.[8]

The Union Restored

The Civil War ended at different times in 1865 in various theaters of the war. General Robert E. Lee surrendered his Army of Northern Virginia, the principal Confederate army in the eastern theater, to General Ulysses S. Grant at Appomattox Court House, Virginia, on April 9. The next day, after the country had endured four long years of civil war, the *New York Times* headlines were simple but emphatic:

UNION

—

VICTORY!

—

PEACE!

Surrender of General Lee and His Whole Army.[9]

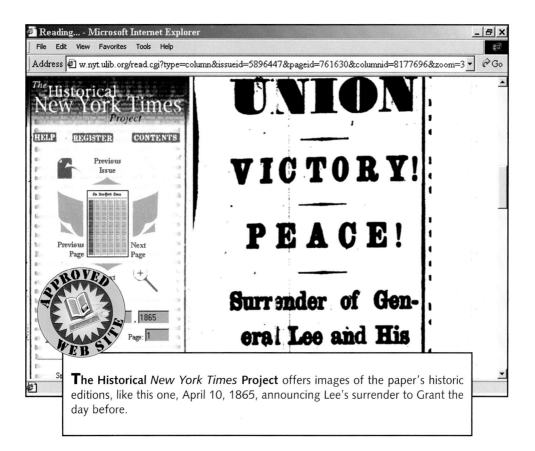

The Historical *New York Times* Project offers images of the paper's historic editions, like this one, April 10, 1865, announcing Lee's surrender to Grant the day before.

A few days later, General Joseph E. Johnston surrendered the Army of Tennessee to General William T. Sherman in Bentonville, North Carolina. It was not until June 2 that General Edmund Kirby Smith, at Galveston, Texas, surrendered the remaining Confederate troops.[10]

A Day of Gloom

Despite the victory, supporters of the Union were saddened by the assassination of its president, Abraham Lincoln, and the wounding of other officials on April 14. Lincoln died the next morning. The *New York Times* edition of April 16 with news of the president's death

The Gettysburg Address

Access this Web site from http://www.myreportlinks.com

President Abraham Lincoln delivered a two-minute address in November 1863 that has become one of the most famous speeches in American history. This Library of Congress site includes drafts of the Gettysburg Address as well as the only known photograph of the president on that day.

featured vertical bold black lines, symbols of mourning, between columns.

> **The President's body was removed from the private residence opposite Ford's Theatre to the executive mansion this morning at 9:30 o'clock, in a hearse, and wrapped in the American flag. It was escorted by a small guard of cavalry. . . .**
>
> **A dense crowd accompanied the remains to the White House, where a military guard excluded the crowd, allowing none but persons of the household and personal friends of the deceased to enter the premises. . . .**
>
> **The bells are tolling mournfully. All is the deepest gloom and sadness. Strong men weep in the streets. The grief is wide-spread and deep and in strange contrast to the joy so lately manifested over our recent military victories.**
>
> **This is indeed a day of gloom.**[11]

The Union was to be restored, but its great wartime chieftain would not be present to lead it through Reconstruction.

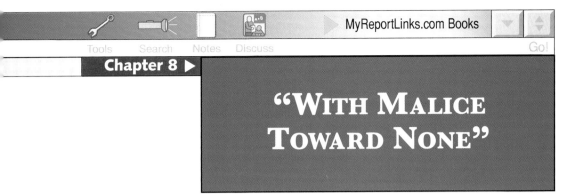
Chapter 8 ▶

"WITH MALICE TOWARD NONE"

The Civil War resulted from long-standing differences between the majority of citizens of Northern and Southern states over how to interpret the United States Constitution. Southerners generally supported the states' rights theory, meaning that the will of a state's residents

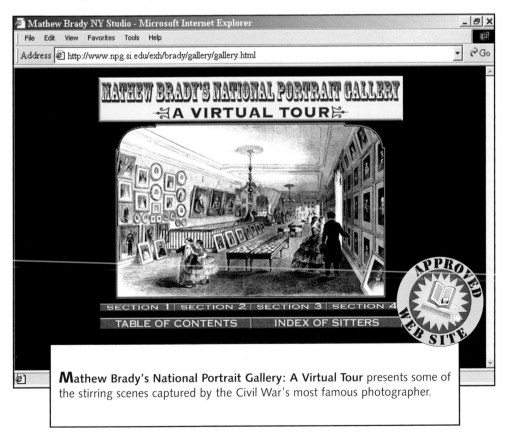

Mathew Brady's National Portrait Gallery: A Virtual Tour presents some of the stirring scenes captured by the Civil War's most famous photographer.

should prevail within its borders where the Constitution did not strictly prohibit it or clearly give a specific power to the federal government.

Northerners generally supported the "We the people" theory, referring to the first three words of the preamble to the Constitution. They believed that the will of the majority in the Union as a whole should prevail through-out that Union unless the Constitution assigned a specific power to states.

Southerners and Northerners found much to dispute between 1789 and 1860, but slavery divided the sections most severely. Southerners generally believed slavery a matter for the citizens of each state to decide for them-selves. Most Northerners, meanwhile, believed that the evil of slavery could and should be addressed by the entire nation—and eliminated.

The Divide Widens

From 1845 until the presidential election in 1860, the divide between Southerners and Northerners widened until the election itself caused seven states to secede. They withdrew to preserve what they believed was each state's right to allow slavery.

After a military clash over possession of Fort Sumter in Charleston in mid-April 1861, President Abraham Lincoln called for seventy-five thousand volunteers to shoulder arms to deal with the "insurrection" in South Carolina. This caused the secession of four more states.

Delegates from the seceded states formed the Confederate States of America and prepared to defend

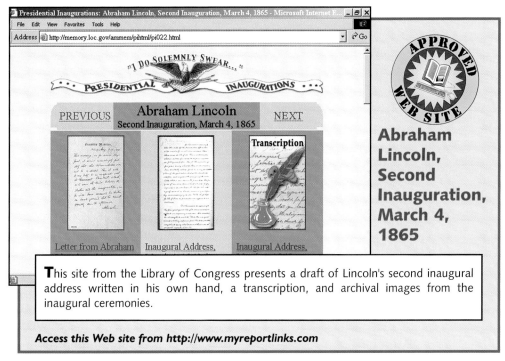

Presidential Inaugurations: Abraham Lincoln, Second Inauguration, March 4, 1865 - Microsoft Internet E...

File Edit View Favorites Tools Help

Address http://memory.loc.gov/ammem/pihtml/pi022.html

"I DO SOLEMNLY SWEAR..."
PRESIDENTIAL INAUGURATIONS

PREVIOUS   **Abraham Lincoln**
Second Inauguration, March 4, 1865   NEXT

Transcription

Letter from Abraham   Inaugural Address,   Inaugural Address,

Abraham Lincoln, Second Inauguration, March 4, 1865

This site from the Library of Congress presents a draft of Lincoln's second inaugural address written in his own hand, a transcription, and archival images from the inaugural ceremonies.

Access this Web site from http://www.myreportlinks.com

themselves from any efforts to make them return to the Union. Meanwhile, the Union continued to enlarge its military force for just that mission.

Slavery remained the fundamental issue between the North and the South, but neither side could have raised an army only to end or defend the South's "peculiar institution," as slavery was sometimes called. So preserving the Union became the first commitment of the Lincoln administration. Lincoln summarized this in his second inaugural address in March 1865:

> On the occasion corresponding to this four years ago, all thoughts were anxiously directed to an impending civil war. All dreaded it—all sought to avert it. While the inaugural address was being delivered from this place, devoted altogether to saving the Union without war, insurgent agents

were in the city seeking to *destroy* it without war—seeking
to dissol[v]e the Union, and divide effects, by negotiation.
Both parties deprecated war; but one of them would *make*
war rather than let the nation survive; and the other would
accept war rather than let it perish. And the war came.[1]

Most Southerners responded to their new government's call to arms to defend their country from
Northern invasion. Ending slavery everywhere did not
become a commitment in the North until after Lincoln
issued the preliminary Emancipation Proclamation in
September 1863. Slavery did not end legally until the
Thirteenth Amendment to the Constitution was ratified
on December 6, 1865.

Anticipating a successful conclusion to the war, Lincoln
ended his second inaugural address in a spirit of friendship toward the South:

With malice toward none; with charity for all; with firmness
in the right, as God gives us to see the right, let us strive on
to finish the work we are in; to bind up the nation's wounds;
to care for him who shall have borne the battle, and for his
widow, and his orphan—to do all which may achieve and
cherish a just, and a lasting peace, among ourselves, and
with all nations.[2]

▶ "And the War Came"

The Civil War proved costly in dollars and even more so
in human life. The federal budget increased from approximately $60 million in 1860 to more than $1 billion by

the end of the war. The Confederacy's costs of financing the war are not known, but must have been in the millions of dollars. The U.S. armed forces increased from approximately sixteen thousand men when the war began to more than 2 million men during the four years of war. Another 800,000 or so served in the Confederate army.

In total, nearly one million men died and were wounded in military service as a result of the Civil War. That included those who perished from disease and the inability of the medical profession to deal with wounds, which almost always introduced infection in addition to the wound itself. Most severe wounds to arms or legs resulted in amputation, while wounds to the abdomen were usually fatal.

An Address at Gettysburg

Nowhere in a single battle were more lives lost than on the battlefields of Gettysburg, with more than 23,000 Union casualties and more than 28,000 Confederate casualties.

In November of that year, President Abraham Lincoln was invited to speak at the dedication of a national cemetery at Gettysburg where many of the Union soldiers were buried. Lincoln was not the featured speaker, however. That honor fell to Edward Everett, perhaps the most famous orator of the time, and he spoke for two hours. Lincoln followed with a speech that lasted only two minutes. That two-minute address, however, is considered by many historians to be the most eloquent and

△ An excerpt from the Gettysburg Address, in Lincoln's handwriting.

important speech in American history. In it, Lincoln went beyond the significance of the battle itself to make a broader statement about the significance of the entire war and its meaning for the future of the nation. The following is a draft of the address that some scholars believe to be Lincoln's original draft.

Four score and seven years ago our fathers brought forth, upon this continent, a new nation, conceived in liberty, and dedicated to the proposition that "all men are created equal."

Now we are engaged in a great civil war, testing whether that nation, or any nation so conceived, and so dedicated, can long endure. We are met on a great battle field of that war. We have come to dedicate a portion of it, as a final resting place for those who died here, that the nation might live. This we may, in all propriety do. But, in a larger sense, we can not dedicate—we can not consecrate—we can not hallow, this ground—The brave men, living and dead, who struggled here, have hallowed it, far above our poor power to add or detract. The world will little note, nor long remember what we say here; while it can never forget what they did here.

It is rather for us, the living, we here be dedicated to the great task remaining before us—that, from these honored dead we take increased devotion to that cause for which they here, gave the last full measure of devotion—that we here highly resolve these dead shall not have died in vain; that the nation, shall have a new birth of freedom, and that government of the people by the people for the people, shall not perish from the earth.[3]

Other Casualties of War

During America's Civil War, soldiers were not the only ones to suffer. Civilians in the path of war lost their lives and also their property—some from confiscation by their own government, the opposing army,

Ulysses S. Grant (photographed here in 1864) offered generous terms of surrender to the soldiers of Lee's army.

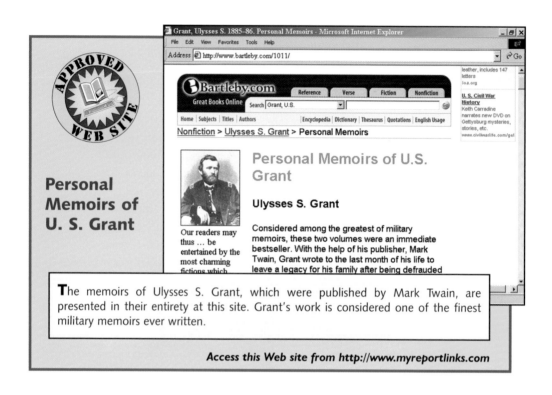

Grant, Ulysses S. 1885–86. Personal Memoirs - Microsoft Internet Explorer

Personal Memoirs of U. S. Grant

The memoirs of Ulysses S. Grant, which were published by Mark Twain, are presented in their entirety at this site. Grant's work is considered one of the finest military memoirs ever written.

Access this Web site from http://www.myreportlinks.com

or because they could no longer farm or produce the things they once did. This was especially true of Pennsylvanians during the Gettysburg campaign; Georgians and South Carolinians during General William T. Sherman's march from Atlanta to Savannah, then northward through the Carolinas in 1864 and 1865; and Virginians throughout the war.[4]

And the War Ended

By early April, it was apparent to Robert E. Lee that the "overwhelming numbers and resources" of the Union army could not be resisted further with any hope of success. General Lee visited with General Grant, commander of the Army of the Potomac, in Appomattox Court House,

Virginia, on April 9, 1865, to discuss surrendering his army. Grant received Lee cordially and, as Grant's formal written response to Lee indicated, allowed generous terms of surrender:

> Gen: In accordance with the substance of my letter to you of the 8th inst., I propose to receive the surrender of the Army of N. Va. on the following terms, to wit: Rolls of all the officers and men to be made in duplicate. One copy to be given to an officer designated by me, the other to be retained by such officer or officers as you may designate. The officers to give their individual paroles not to take up arms against the Government of the United States until properly exchanged, and each company or regimental commander sign a like parole for the men of their commands. The arms, artillery and public property to be parked and stacked, and turned over to the officer appointed by me to receive them. This will not embrace the side-arms of the officers, nor their private horses or baggage. This done, each officer and man will be allowed to return to their homes, not to be disturbed by United States authority so long as they observe their paroles and the laws in force where they may reside.[5]

Lee's men stacked their arms, as required by the terms of surrender, and made their way home. They faced an uncertain future, and although sectional differences remained, one thing was certain: the Union. Nearly a century and a half later, there is still one United States of America.

Report Links

The Internet sites described below can be accessed at
http://www.myreportlinks.com

▶**The Valley of the Shadow: Two Communities in the American Civil War**
Editor's Choice Learn about two communities during the Civil War.

▶**Documenting the American South: The Southern Homefront, 1861–1865**
Editor's Choice Learn about life in the South during the Civil War from primary sources.

▶**Selected Civil War Photographs**
Editor's Choice Take a look at Civil War photographs.

▶**The Civil War**
Editor's Choice This PBS site takes a look at the Civil War.

▶**Primary Sources: Civil War Effects**
Editor's Choice This site focuses on the impact of the Civil War in Kentucky.

▶**CivilWar@Smithsonian: Collections**
Editor's Choice View the Smithsonian Institution's collection of Civil War artifacts.

▶**Abraham Lincoln, Second Inauguration, March 4, 1865**
This Library of Congress site presents the second inaugural address of Abraham Lincoln.

▶**American Civil War Collections at the Electronic Text Center**
Letters and other primary sources from the Civil War are included in this site.

▶**American Visionaries: Frederick Douglass**
Visit the home of abolitionist Frederick Douglass.

▶**Antietam National Battlefield Image Gallery**
View photographic and painted images of Antietam.

▶**Appomattox Court House**
See where the Civil War came to an end.

▶**Assassination of President Abraham Lincoln**
The president is shot.

▶**The Avalon Project: Confederate States of America Documents**
Read documents from the Confederate States of America.

▶**Civil War: Soldiers & Sailors System**
Learn about the soldiers and sailors who fought in the Civil War.

▶**The Civil War Home Page**
View a collection of Civil War resources.

Report Links

The Internet sites described below can be accessed at
http://www.myreportlinks.com

▶**Crisis at Fort Sumter**
Learn about the war's first conflict.

▶**Featured Documents: The Emancipation Proclamation**
Read President Lincoln's Emancipation Proclamation.

▶**The Gettysburg Address**
View drafts of Lincoln's Gettysburg Address.

▶**Gettysburg National Military Park**
The pivotal battle of the war is fought in Pennsylvania.

▶**The Historical *New York Times* Project: The Civil War Years, 1860–1866**
View original newspaper accounts of the Civil War.

▶**A House Divided: America in the Age of Lincoln**
The United States and its leader during the Civil War are examined in this site.

▶**Jump Back in Time: Civil War (1860–1865)**
This Library of Congress site takes a look at the Civil War through primary sources.

▶**The Library of Congress: Civil War Maps**
View a collection of Civil War maps.

▶**Mathew Brady's National Portrait Gallery: A Virtual Tour**
Browse Mathew Brady photographs at this site.

▶**Music of the Civil War**
Learn about the songs that boosted soldiers' spirits during the Civil War.

▶**The Papers of Jefferson Davis**
View the papers of Confederate leader Jefferson Davis.

▶**Personal Memoirs of U.S. Grant**
Read the memoirs of the Union's leading general.

▶**Poetry and Music of the War Between the States**
Take a look at some of the poems and songs created during America's Civil War.

▶**The Robert E. Lee Papers at Washington & Lee University**
View original documents written by the Confederacy's leading general at this university site.

▶**Virginia Military Institute Archives: Civil War Resources**
View images and documents from the Confederacy at this military academy Web site.

adjutant general—The chief administrative officer of an army or a major military division.

ammunition—Bullets or balls fired from rifles or cannons during a battle.

arduous—Describing a task or an accomplishment that has been achieved through great difficulty.

armies—The largest military units of the war, composed of more than one corps, such as the Army of Northern Virginia (Confederate) and the Army of the Potomac (Union).

artillery—Large weapons, such as cannons, that can be transported; also an army unit that mans such weapons.

brigade—A group of soldiers that is made up of two or more regiments.

casualties—Losses during war due to death, wounds, disease, imprisonment, or from going missing in action.

cavalry—Soldiers on horseback.

civilians—Non-military persons or activities.

company—The basic unit of infantry in the army, usually composed of approximately one hundred soldiers commanded by a captain.

conscription—The mandatory enrollment of civilians in the military.

corps—An army unit made up of two or more divisions.

currency—paper money (such as dollar bills).

division—A large military unit made up of several regiments or brigades. Two or more divisions make up a corps.

emancipation—Freedom from bondage, or the freeing of people who had been enslaved.

ferriage—The toll charged to take a ferry.

infantry—An army unit made up of soldiers that fight on foot.

maneuvering—Moving soldiers into position to achieve an advantage before a battle occurs.

mercenaries—Soldiers who enlist in an army to receive pay rather than commitment to the army's cause.

morale—The level of enthusiasm, confidence, or loyalty of a group (such as soldiers) for a task (such as their service).

obligation—Duty or responsibility.

obstruct—To interfere with or keep from happening.

proclamation—A statement of policy or purpose issued by a civilian or military authority.

provisional—temporary.

quartermaster—The officer in charge of supplying troops with their needs.

Reconstruction—The period in American history following the Civil War, from 1866 to 1877. Reconstruction as put in place by Congress involved bringing the former Confederate states back into the Union, rebuilding the South after the war's destruction, and providing some help to newly freed African Americans.

regiment—An army unit larger than a company but smaller than a division.

secession—In United States history, the act of Southern states in leaving the Union.

segregation—The separation of races. For a long period in American history, in certain places, African Americans were not allowed to use the same public facilities (schools, restaurants, and so on) as white people.

songsters—Little books of song lyrics carried by soldiers.

states' rights—The principle based on the Tenth Amendment to the United States Constitution that says powers not given to the federal government and not prohibited by it to the states are reserved for the states. In the years leading up to the American Civil War, most states' rights advocates in the South believed that the federal government had no right to restrict the spread of slavery to new states or territories.

theater of war—An area or a region in which a war is conducted.

typhoid fever—An infectious disease resulting in high fevers and intestinal illness caused by a bacterium. The disease, which can result in death, was common in the camps during the war because of unsanitary conditions.

valor—Personal bravery; often used to describe acts of heroism in war.

volley—The discharge of weapons at the same time.

Chapter 1. "A Fearful Shock": Three Pivotal Days at Gettysburg

1. Robert E. Lee, "Lee's Farewell to His Army," April 10, 1865, from *Recollections and Letters of General Lee, by Captain R.E. Lee, his Son,* p. 153, as quoted in *Documents of American History,* 8th ed., Henry Steele Commager, ed. (New York: Appleton-Century-Crofts, 1968), p. 447. Reproduced with permission of the copyright holder.

2. J. Gregory Acken, ed., *Inside the Army of the Potomac: The Civil War Experience of Captain Francis Adams Donaldson* (Mechanicsburg, Pa.: Stackpole Books, 1998), p. 288. Used with permission of Stackpole Books.

3. Archie P. McDonald, ed., *Make Me a Map of the Valley: The Civil War Journal of Stonewall Jackson's Topographer* (Dallas: Southern Methodist University Press, 1973), pp. 156–157.

4. Joseph Rosengarten, "Buford and Reynolds Hold Up the Confederate Advance," in *The Blue and the Gray: The Story of the Civil War As Told By Participants,* Henry Steele Commager, ed. (New York: Fairfax Press, 1982), p. 601. Reproduced with permission of the copyright holder.

5. "These Were Bitter Days," Sallie Myers' Account of Gettysburg, Voices of Battle, Gettysburg National Military Park Web site, first published as "How a Gettysburg Schoolteacher Spent Her Vacation in 1863," *The Sunday Call,* San Francisco, California.

6. Ibid.

7. Theodore Gerrish, "Army Life," in *The Blue and the Gray,* Henry Steele Commager, ed., p. 620. Reproduced with permission of the copyright holder.

8. James Longstreet, "From Manassas to Appomattox," in *The Blue and the Gray,* Henry Steele Commager, ed., p. 630. Reproduced with permission of the copyright holder.

9. Jedediah Hotchkiss in McDonald, p. 158.

Chapter 2. A House Divided: A Brief History of the Civil War

1. James M. McPherson, *Ordeal By Fire: The Civil War and Reconstruction,* 2nd ed. (New York: McGraw-Hill, 1992), p. 2.

2. J.G. Randall and David Donald, *The Civil War and Reconstruction,* 2nd ed. (Lexington, Mass.: D.C. Heath & Company, 1969), pp. 78–105.

3. Archie P. McDonald, *Texas: All Hail the Mighty State,* 3rd ed. (Austin: Eakin Press, 2004), pp. 138–140.

4. McPherson, pp. 141–142.

5. Randall and Donald, pp. 160–161.

6. The best account of the bombardment of Fort Sumter is W.A. Swanberg's *First Blood: The Story of Fort Sumter* (New York: Charles Scribner's Sons, 1957). For a brief account, see James I. Robertson, *The Concise Illustrated History of the Civil War* (Harrisburg, Pa.: Stackpole Books, 1971), pp. 11–12.

7. McPherson, pp. 162–166.

8. For a review of the role of Tredegar Iron Works, see Robert H. Jones, *Disrupted Decades: The Civil War and Reconstruction Years* (New York: Charles Scribner's Sons, 1973), p. 232. For a brief biography of Josiah Gorgas, see "Gorgas, Josiah," in *Dictionary of American Biography,* Allan Johnson and Dumas Malone, eds. (New York: Charles Scribner's Sons, 1960), pp. 428–430.

9. McPherson, pp. 201–202.

10. Abraham Lincoln, First Inaugural Address, Final Version, March 1861, The Abraham Lincoln Papers at the Library of Congress, Series 1. General Correspondence. 1833–1916, Manuscript Division (Washington, D.C.: American Memory Project, 2000–2002), <http://memory.loc.gov/ammem/alhtml/alhome.html> (May 5, 2005).

11. McPherson, pp. 272–273, 357.

12. Ibid., pp. 203–207.

13. James I. Robertson, *The Concise Illustrated History of the Civil War* (Harrisburg, Pa.: Stackpole Books, 1971), pp. 18–23. Used with permission of Stackpole Books.

14. Robert E. Lee, "Lee's Farewell to His Army," April 10, 1865, from *Recollections and Letters of General Lee, by Captain R.E. Lee, his Son,* p. 153, as quoted in *Documents of American History,* 8th ed., Henry Steele Commager, ed. (New York: Appleton-Century-Crofts, 1968), p. 447. Reproduced with permission of the copyright holder.

Chapter 3. In the Words of Union Soldiers

1. James M. McPherson, *What They Fought For, 1861–1865* (Baton Rouge: Louisiana State University Press, 1994), p. 7.

2. Robert F. Harris and John Niflot, comps., *Dear Sister: The Civil War Letters of the Brothers Gould* (Westport, Conn.: Praeger, 1998), pp. 1–2. Copyright © 1998 by Robert F. Harris and John Niflot. Reproduced with permission of Greenwood Publishing Group, Inc., Westport, CT.

3. Robert F. Harris and John Niflot, comps., *Dear Sister: The Civil War Letters of the Brothers Gould* (Westport, Conn.: Praeger, 1998), pp. 1–2. Copyright © 1998 by Robert F. Harris and John Niflot. Reproduced with permission of Greenwood Publishing Group, Inc., Westport, CT.

4. A letter from Charles Douglass (son) to Frederick Douglass, July 6, 1863, Frederick Douglass Papers, Library of Congress, Manuscript Division, <http://memory.loc.gov/ammem/aaohtml/exhibit/aopart4.html#04c> (June 6, 2005).

5. Coralou Peel Lassen, ed., *Dear Sarah: Letters Home from a Soldier of the Iron Brigade* (Bloomington: Indiana University Press, 1999), p. 7. Used with permission of Indiana University.

6. Coralou Peel Lassen, ed., *Dear Sarah: Letters Home from a Soldier of the Iron Brigade* (Bloomington: Indiana University Press, 1999), p. 8. Used with permission of Indiana University.

7. Lauren Cook Burgess, ed., *An Uncommon Soldier, The Civil War Letters of Sarah Rosetta Wakeman, alias Pvt. Lyons Wakeman, 153rd Regiment, New York State Volunteers, 1862–1864,* Pasadena, MD: The Minerva Center, Inc. (New York: Oxford University Press, 1994), p. 18.

8. Lauren Cook Burgess, ed., *An Uncommon Soldier, The Civil War Letters of Sarah Rosetta Wakeman, alias Pvt. Lyons Wakeman, 153rd Regiment, New York State Volunteers, 1862–1864,* Pasadena, MD: The Minerva Center, Inc. (New York: Oxford University Press, 1994), p. 46.

9. Lauren Cook Burgess, ed., *An Uncommon Soldier, The Civil War Letters of Sarah Rosetta Wakeman, alias Pvt. Lyons Wakeman, 153rd Regiment, New York State Volunteers, 1862–1864,* Pasadena, MD: The Minerva Center, Inc. (New York: Oxford University Press, 1994), pp. 12–13.

10. Eric J. Wittenberg, ed., *"We Have It Damn Hard Out Here," The Civil War Letters of Sergeant Thomas W. Smith, 6th Pennsylvania Cavalry* (Kent, Ohio: Kent State University Press, 1999), pp. 9–10. Used with permission of Kent State University Press.

11. "General Orders, No. 8 by command of Brig. Gen. A.E. Burnside," in *The War of the Rebellion: A Compilation of the Official Records of the Union and Confederate Armies* (Washington: Government Printing Office, 1883), series I, vol. IX, p. 363.

12. Robert F. Harris and John Niflot, comps., *Dear Sister: The Civil War Letters of the Brothers Gould* (Westport, Conn.: Praeger, 1998), pp. 153–154. Copyright © 1998 by Robert F. Harris and John Niflot. Reproduced with permission of Greenwood Publishing Group, Inc., Westport, CT.

Chapter 4. In the Words of Confederate Soldiers

1. Rev. J. Wm. Jones, D.D., *Christ in the Camp; or, Religion in Lee's Army* (Waco, Tex.: James E. Yeager, Publisher, 1887), p. 18.

2. Douglas Southall Freeman, *R.E. Lee: A Biography, vol. 1* (New York: Charles Scribner's Sons, 1934), p. 443.

3. Elizabeth Whitley Roberson, ed., *In Care Of Yellow River: The Complete Civil War Letters of Pvt. Eli Pinson Landers to His Mother* (Gretna, La.: Pelican Publishing Co., 1997), p. 18. Reprinted with permission of Pelican Publishing Co.

4. Elizabeth Whitley Roberson, ed., *In Care Of Yellow River: The Complete Civil War Letters of Pvt. Eli Pinson Landers to His Mother* (Gretna, La.: Pelican Publishing Co., 1997), p. 18. Reprinted with permission of Pelican Publishing Co.

5. Elizabeth Whitley Roberson, ed., *In Care Of Yellow River: The Complete Civil War Letters of Pvt. Eli Pinson Landers to His Mother* (Gretna, La.: Pelican Publishing Co., 1997), p. 51. Reprinted with permission of Pelican Publishing Co.

6. Elizabeth Whitley Roberson, ed., *In Care Of Yellow River: The Complete Civil War Letters of Pvt. Eli Pinson Landers to His Mother* (Gretna, La.: Pelican Publishing Co., 1997), p. 18. Reprinted with permission of Pelican Publishing Co.

7. Jeffrey C. Lowe and Sam Hodges, eds., *Letters to Amanda: The Civil War Letters of Marion Hill Fitzpatrick, Army of Northern Virginia* (Macon, Ga.: Mercer University Press, 1998), p. 5.

8. Ibid., p. 76.

9. Ann K. Blomquist and Robert A. Taylor, eds., *This Cruel War: The Civil War Letters of Grant and Malinda Taylor, 1862–1865* (Macon, Ga.: Mercer University Press, 2000), p. 1.

10. Ibid., pp. 144–145.

11. Eddy R. Parker, ed., *Touched By Fire: Letters From Company D, 5th Texas Infantry, Hood's Brigade, Army of Northern Virginia, 1862–1865* (Hillsboro, Tex.: Hill College Press, 2000), p. 34.

12. George F. Montgomery, Jr., ed., *Georgia Sharpshooter: The Civil War Diary and Letters of William Rhadamanthus Montgomery* (Macon, Ga.: Mercer University Press, 1997), p. 77.

13. Ibid.

14. Jones, pp. 355–356.

15. Blomquist and Taylor, p. 143.

16. Lowe and Hodges, p. 209.

Chapter 5. The War in the Words of Civilians

1. Mary Boykin Chesnut, *A Diary from Dixie, as Written by Mary Boykin Chesnut, Wife of James Chesnut, Jr., United States Senator from South Carolina, 1859–1861, and Afterward an Aide to Jefferson Davis and a Brigadier-General in the Confederate Army.* (New York: D. Appleton and Company, 1905), p. 35.

2. Ibid., p. 38.

3. George Templeton Strong, quoted in Glenn M. Linden and Thomas J. Pressly, *Voices From the House Divided: The United States Civil War As Personal Experience* (New York: McGraw Hill, 1995), p. 8. Reproduced with the permission of The McGraw-Hill Companies.

4. George Templeton Strong, quoted in Glenn M. Linden and Thomas J. Pressly, *Voices From the House Divided: The United States Civil War As Personal Experience* (New York: McGraw Hill, 1995), p. 9. Reproduced with the permission of The McGraw-Hill Companies.

5. William Howard Russell, *My Diary North and South,* (Boston: T.O.H.P. Burnham, 1863), pp. 37–38.

6. Ibid., p. 173.

7. Clement L. Vallandigham, *The Record of Hon. C.L. Vallandigham on Abolition, the Union, and the Civil War* (Cincinnati, 1863), pp. 180–199, quoted in Avery Craven, Walter Johnson, and F. Roger Dunn, *A Documentary History of the American People* (Boston: Ginn and Company, 1951), p. 415.

8. John B. Jones, quoted in Henry Steele Commager, ed., *The Blue and the Gray: The Story of the Civil War As Told By Participants* (New York: Fairfax Press, 1982), p. 745. Reproduced with permission of the copyright holder.

9. Maria Daly, quoted in Glenn M. Linden and Thomas J. Pressly, *Voices From the House Divided: The United States Civil War As Personal Experience* (New York: McGraw Hill, 1995), p. 254. Reproduced with the permission of The McGraw-Hill Companies.

10. Frederick Douglass, quoted in Glenn M. Linden and Thomas J. Pressly, *Voices From the House Divided: The United States Civil War As Personal Experience* (New York: McGraw Hill, 1995), p. 260. Reproduced with the permission of The McGraw-Hill Companies.

11. Chesnut, p. 389.

12. Ibid., p. 390.

13. Ibid.

Chapter 6. The War in Song

1. Wayne Erbsen, *Rousing Songs and True Tales of the Civil War* (Asheville, N.C.: Native Ground Music, 1999), pp. 4–6.

2. "The Bonnie Blue Flag," Lyrics by Harry Macarthy, n.d., <http://www.civilwarpoetry.org/confederate/songs/bonnie.html> (August 25, 2005).

3. Maryland at a Glance, State Symbols, Maryland State Song— "Maryland, My Maryland," n.d., <http://www.mdarchives.state.md.us/msa/mdmanual/01glance/html/symbols/lyrics.html> (August 25, 2005).

4. Irwin Silber, comp. and ed., *Songs of the Civil War* (New York: Columbia University Press, 1960), p. 55.

5. New Jersey Public Library, The Civil War: Rhythms & Rhymes, Songs, "Dixie," n.d., <http://www.njpublib.org/cwsongs.html> (August 26, 2005).

6. Historic American Sheet Music, "Battle Cry of Freedom," Digital Scriptorium, Rare Book, Manuscript, and Special Collections Library, Duke University, n.d., <http://scriptorium.lib.duke.edu/sheetmusic/lyrics/Root__Battle_cry_of_freedom.html> (May 15, 2005).

7. Silber, pp. 8–9.

8. Civil War Poetry, "Marching Through Georgia" by Henry Clay Work, n.d., <http://www.civilwarpoetry.org/union/songs/marchga.html> (October 20, 2005).

9. Silber, pp. 10–11.

10. "The Battle Hymn of the Republic" by Julia Ward Howe, n.d., <http://usinfo.state.gov/usa/infousa/facts/symbols/bathymn.htm> (August 26, 2005).

11. Vicksburg National Military Park, Louisiana/Mississippi, Camp Life, "Goober Peas," n.d., <http://www.nps.gov/vick/edugide/chp_2/goobrpea.htm> (August 26, 2005).

12. Civil War Music at the Gettysburg National Military Park Kidzpage! "Just Before the Battle, Mother," by George F. Root, n.d., <http://www.nps.gov/gett/gettkidz/gkmusic/cwsong2.htm> (August 26, 2005).

Chapter 7. Press Coverage and Official Accounts of the War

1. T. Harry Williams, Richard N. Current, and Frank Freidel, *A History of the United States to 1876* (New York: Alfred A. Knopf, 1960), pp. 525–526.

2. J.G. Randall and David Donald, *The Civil War and Reconstruction,* 2nd ed. (Lexington. Mass.: D.C. Heath and Company, 1969), pp. 495–496.

3. The *Charleston Mercury,* April 15, 1865, p. 1, quoted in Eugene P. Moehring and Arleen Keylin, *The Civil War Extra, From the Pages of The Charleston Mercury & The New York Times* (New York: Arno Press, 1975), p. 14.

4. The *Charleston Mercury,* April 15, 1861, p. 14, Ibid.

5. The *New York Times,* April 15, 1861, p. 1, Ibid., p. 15.

6. The *Charleston Mercury,* May 13, 1863, Ibid., p. 178.

7. The *New York Times,* May 8, 1863, p. 1, Ibid., p. 177.

8. The *New York Times,* September 22, 1864, Ibid., p. 266.

9. The *New York Times,* April 10, 1865, Ibid., p. 302.

10. James I. Robertson, *The Concise Illustrated History of the Civil War* (Harrisburg, Pa.: Stackpole Books, 1971), p. 104. Used with permission of Stackpole Books.

11. *The New York Times,* April 16, 1865, as quoted in Moehring and Keylin, p. 307.

Chapter 8. "With Malice Toward None"

1. Abraham Lincoln, Second Inaugural Address; endorsed by Lincoln, April 10, 1865, March 4, 1865; Series 3, General Correspondence, 1837–1897; The Abraham Lincoln Papers at the Library of Congress, Manuscript Division (Washington, D.C.: American Memory Project, 2000–2002), <http://memory.loc.gov/ammem/alhtml/alhome.html> (May 5, 2005).

2. Ibid.

3. Abraham Lincoln, Gettysburg Address, delivered November 19, 1863; General Correspondence, 1837–1897; The Abraham Lincoln Papers at the Library of Congress, Manuscript Division (Washington, D.C.: American Memory Project, 2000–2002), <http://memory.loc.gov/ammem/alhtml/alhome.html> (May 5, 2005).

4. For summaries of public finance, manpower, and medicine in the Civil War, see James M. McPherson, *Ordeal By Fire: The Civil War and Reconstruction* (New York: McGraw Hill, 1992), pp. 184–186, 201–207; see also James I. Robertson, *Soldiers Blue and Grey* (Columbia: University of South Carolina Press, 1988), pp. 145–169.

5. U.S. Grant, *Personal Memoirs of U.S. Grant,* vol. II (New York: Charles L. Webster & Company, 1886), pp. 491–492.

Further Reading

Anderson, Dale. *A Soldier's Life in the Civil War.* Milwaukee: World Almanac Library, 2004.

Archer, Jules. *A House Divided: The Lives of Ulysses S. Grant and Robert E. Lee.* New York: Scholastic, 1995.

Arnold, James R., and Roberta Wiener. *Life Goes On: The Civil War at Home, 1861–1865.* Minneapolis: Lerner Publications Co., 2002.

Ashby, Ruth, ed. *The Diary of Sam Watkins, a Confederate Soldier.* Tarrytown, N.Y.: Benchmark Books, 2003.

Burgess, Lauren Cook, ed. *An Uncommon Soldier: The Civil War Letters of Sarah Rosetta Wakeman, Alias Pvt. Lyons Wakeman, 153rd Regiment, New York State Volunteers, 1862–1864.* New York: Oxford University Press, 1994.

Haskins, Jim. *Black, Blue & Gray: African Americans in the Civil War.* New York: Simon & Schuster Books for Young Readers, 1998.

Malone, Margaret Gay, ed. *The Diary of Susie King Taylor, Civil War Nurse.* New York: Benchmark Books, 2003.

Marrin, Albert A. *Commander in Chief: Abraham Lincoln and the Civil War.* New York: Dutton, 1997.

McPherson, James M. *Fields of Fury: the American Civil War.* New York: Atheneum Books for Young Readers, 2002.

O'Connell, Kim A. *Major Battles of the Civil War.* Berkeley Heights, N.J.: MyReportLinks.com Books, 2004.

Silverman, Jerry. *Songs and Stories of the Civil War.* Brookfield, Conn.: Twenty-First Century Books, 2002.

Tanaka, Shelley. *Gettysburg: The Legendary Battle and the Address That Inspired a Nation.* New York: Hyperion Books for Children, 2003.